The Collaborative School

A Work Environment for Effective Instruction

Stuart C. Smith and James J. Scott

ERIC

Clearinghouse on Educational Management
University of Oregon

National Association of Secondary School Principals

ISBN 0-86552-092-5
Library of Congress Catalog Card Number: 87-81544
ERIC/CEM School Management Digest Series, Number 33
ERIC/CEM Accession Number: EA 021 574

ERIC Clearinghouse on Educational Management
University of Oregon
1787 Agate Street
Eugene, OR 97403-5207
(503) 346-5043

National Association of Secondary School Principals
1904 Association Drive
Reston, VA 22091-1598
(703) 860-0200

Design: University Publications, University of Oregon

Printed in the United States of America, 1990

The University of Oregon is an equal opportunity, affirmative action institution. This publication was prepared with funding from the Office of Educational Research and Improvement, U.S. Department of Education under Contract No. OERI-R-86-0003. Points of view or opinions do not necessarily reflect the positions or policies of ERIC, OERI, or the Department of Education. No federal funds were used in the printing of this publication.

Contents

About ERIC

The Educational Resources Information Center (ERIC) is a national information system operated by the U.S. Department of Education. ERIC serves the educational community by disseminating educational research results and other resource information that can be used in developing more effective educational programs.

The ERIC Clearinghouse on Educational Management, one of several such units in the system, was established at the University of Oregon in 1966. The Clearinghouse and its companion units process research results and journal articles for announcement in ERIC's index and abstract bulletins.

Research reports are announced in *Resources in Education (RIE)*, available in many libraries, and by subscription for $51 a year from the United States Government Printing Office, Washington, D.C. 20402.

Most of the documents listed in *RIE* can be purchased through the ERIC Document Reproduction Service, operated by Computer Microfilm International Corporation.

Journal articles are announced in *Current Index to Journals in Education*. *CIJE* is also available in many libraries, and can be ordered for $150 a year from Oryx Press, 2214 North Central at Encanto, Phoenix, Ariz. 85004. Semiannual cumulations can be ordered separately.

In addition to processing documents and journal articles, the Clearinghouse prepares bibliographies, literature reviews, monographs, and other interpretive research studies on topics in its educational area.

Foreword

Collaboration is seldom mentioned in the effective schools literature of the past decade. Nor is it part of the vocabulary of recent national studies of American education. Collaboration appears to be neither part of the problem nor part of the solution when considering reform of public education.

Yet, evidence is accumulating that the nature of the relationships among adults who live and work in schools has a tremendous influence upon the school's quality and character and on the accomplishment of its pupils. Two important tributaries feed this growing knowledge base: social science research, and the craft knowledge of teachers and principals. This book draws upon both as it attempts to illuminate and legitimize collaboration as a critical characteristic of good schools.

The fact that a few schools exist where adults observe one another, communicate, share what they know, share leadership, and talk openly about education is heartening. As Ron Edmonds used to say, "If I can show you one school where it's happening, then it is possible in all schools."

But there are taboos embedded in the culture of schools that make collaborative behavior very difficult to develop. A well-founded belief prevails in many schools that others have potential for hindrance but not help.

I remember as a principal preparing carefully for my first faculty meeting. Wishing to develop a spirit of collaboration, I arranged chairs in circles and encouraged several teachers to contribute. Yet, during the meeting, I found that I was left doing most of the talking while teachers sat quietly, preferring to listen.

A few minutes after the meeting I looked out my office window at the school parking lot and there the *real* faculty meeting was taking place. Little clusters of teachers were abuzz, expressing their ideas about all the subjects on the agenda.

Collaboration in schools does not come easily. Although this book identifies the principal as a promising figure in making schools more collaborative, it is not clear who within the school or outside the school can initiate, encourage, and sustain collegial behavior among teachers and administrators. Just how might teachers, parents, students, and principals move a school from a climate that has been described as one of "emotional toxicity" toward one that respects, honors, and celebrates open professional support and cooperation? By what means? Employing what resources? Enlisting what kinds of energies?

There is good news in the message of this book: Collaboration is being increasingly recognized as not only a desirable but an essential characteristic of an effective school; many schools have made huge strides toward shared leadership and collaboration; and the principal can be a central force in making a school a more collaborative living space.

Yet I must warn of a danger. Those who promote the collaborative school must beware of contributing to yet one more prescription, one more orthodoxy, one more lesson plan, one more "model" that those outside schools will attempt to inflict and those inside schools will attempt to adopt. This seems to be reform the American way. Because teachers and principals within school have insufficient confidence in their own craft knowledge and their own ability to create and implement their own visions for school reform, they are particularly susceptible to prescriptions and solutions offered up by those outside their walls. Whether the model be open classroom, effective schools, Madeline Hunter, or collaborative schools, these foreign conceptions of educational improvement seldom affect the basic culture of a school.

So how then can a basically sound conception such as the one offered here for a collaborative school avoid becoming yet another set of prescriptions, another list to be imposed upon teachers, principals, and students? While collaborative schools offer important, fundamental ideas for improving a school, until those who inhabit the schoolhouse recognize a need for collaboration, devise their own distinctive model for moving toward collaboration, and assume ownership for the huge task of moving themselves toward collaboration, lasting change in the workplace is unlikely to occur.

During a recent visit to a public junior high school, I noticed a sign on the door of the teachers' room: NO STUDENTS ALLOWED. When I asked a teacher about this message she said, "There are *two* rules for this room. That's the written one. The unwritten rule is 'No talking about teaching in the teachers' room'."

I can think of no statement that so well captures both the importance and the difficulty of developing collaboration within a school. If we're serious about helping schools to become places characterized by cooperation, collegiality, and "talking about teaching," I think we must build upon the foundation stones laid by this volume and begin to address a number of tough questions:

- How can the taboo be overcome that prevents teachers from making themselves, their ideas, and their teaching visible to other teachers, to parents, and to administrators?
- How can principals' relationships with other principals, with teachers, and with students be transformed from adversarial and competitive to more collaborative and cooperative?
- How can students learn to work more cooperatively when the reward system and the expectations of parents, teachers, and college admissions officers tilt toward competition?
- What can those outside schools contribute?
- Under what conditions will teachers, parents, students, and principals—most of whom would prefer more collaboration—come to abandon competition and isolation in favor of collaboration and cooperation?

- Finally, once committed to collaboration, what can anyone do to interrupt the embedded, crusty culture of competitive schools and move toward the development of a lasting collaborative school culture?

This volume sets the stage. But it remains for teachers and principals to write the script and play the lead roles.

Roland S. Barth
Senior Lecturer, Codirector
The Principals' Center
Harvard University

Preface

The ERIC Clearinghouse on Educational Management and the National Association of Secondary School Principals are pleased to make this book available for principals, teachers, and others who seek to build collaborative work environments in schools.

This book is an issue in the Clearinghouse's School Management Digest Series, which offers educational leaders essential information on a wide range of critical concerns in education. The goal of this series is improvement of educational practice. Each Digest points up the practical implications of major research findings so that its readers might better grasp and apply knowledge useful for the operation of the schools.

Stuart C. Smith, the Clearinghouse's director of publications, is coeditor of *School Leadership: Handbook for Excellence* and author of numerous articles and research summaries on topics in educational management.

James J. Scott, commissioned by the Clearinghouse as a research analyst and writer, holds a doctor's degree in English from the University of Oregon.

Timothy J. Dyer
Executive Director
NASSP

Philip K. Piele
Professor and Director
ERIC/CEM

Authors' Preface

"What would a more collaborative school environment look like? What would it take to get it?" These two questions, posed in *Time for Results: The Governors' 1991 Report on Education* in a passage recommending state initiatives to encourage professional school environments, form the rationale for this book.

As the governors' report notes, the benefits of a collaborative work setting—including such practices as mutual help, exchange of ideas, joint planning, and participation in decisions—have been consistently affirmed by studies of effective schools and successful businesses. Yet, if schools are to establish collaborative environments, they need to know what models exist and how to implement them.

Our purpose in these pages is to present evidence showing the benefits of collaboration in schools, to describe a variety of practices and programs already being used by schools that enable their faculties to collaborate, and to show how those practices can be introduced in schools with resources currently available in most school districts.

Our method is simple and detailed presentation of evidence accumulated from the research on these themes and from the accounts of educators themselves who have gained experience with collaboration. Like other publications of the ERIC Clearinghouse on Educational Management, this book uses the technique of "information analysis"—summary and synthesis of the most pertinent ideas from literature and practice. Information from published sources is supplemented with insights and data obtained from telephone interviews and correspondence with educators.

A portion of this book was prepared by the Clearinghouse under subcontract with the North Central Regional Educational Laboratory in Elmhurst, Illinois. Much of the material in Chapters 2 and 5 was published in *From Isolation to Collaboration: Improving the Work Environment of Teaching*, by James J. Scott and Stuart C. Smith. Without the support of the North Central Lab, we would not have been able to include the breadth of literature surveyed here.

Several people (Judith Warren Little, Susan Rosenholtz, Richard Schmuck, Mary Haywood Metz, and Roland Barth) were generous in sending us copies of their publications and offering leads to other sources of information.

We solicited from Roland Barth a perceptive critique that added greatly to the book's depth and coherence. Other helpful comments were provided by Scott Thomson and Tom Koerner of the National Association of Secondary School Principals and Richard Schmuck of the University of Oregon's Division of Educational Policy and Management. We thank Philip Piele for his advice and encouragement throughout the project.

Chapter 1

What Is the Collaborative School?

Consider how the adults in two different kinds of schools interact. In school A, teachers do not discuss with one another their practice of teaching, nor do they help one another to improve their skills. The principal's annual visits to the classrooms to evaluate teachers with the district checklist contribute little to their growth. When administrators initiate new programs, teachers respond with apathy or are uncooperative. Faculty members seldom unite around any effort to improve the school. Most teachers would like increased say in designing the school's instructional program, but a few are content with the status quo.

In contrast to the isolation and fragmentation that characterize school A, teachers in school B feel they are working toward a common goal of school improvement. Teachers observe each other's teaching and strive to help one another improve. Experienced teachers willingly share effective practices with new colleagues.

Asked why they function so well as a team, school B's teachers point to the principal, who engenders in them and their students a vision for the school's success and provides the practical support they need to work together. And they point to each other as resources for solving problems. They are proud to take part in decision making, and they value their control of a portion of the school's instructional budget.

Indications are that most schools in this country have more in common with school A than with school B. Prestigious groups such as the Carnegie Task Force on Teaching as a Profession and the National Governors' Association have drawn attention to several key defects in the typical school's structure: overreliance on bureaucratic rules and regulations, school environments that isolate teachers, evaluation systems that fail to facilitate instructional improvement, lack of teacher involvement in decision making, and obstacles to cooperation between teachers and administrators.

Propelled by a growing awareness of these problems, a consensus is developing among policy makers, researchers, professional organizations representing teachers and administrators, and friends of education in the business community. Educators are experimenting with a variety of alternatives, all of which accord teachers greater respect as professionals at the same time they induce teachers to cooperate with one another and with administrators on school improvement. These new practices and structures—characteristic of school B—all fit in the broad category of what we term the *collaborative school.*

The collaborative school is not new in theory or in practice. The principles of consultation and teamwork have been advocated by management experts for years, and have been successfully applied in the business world. And many characteristics of collaborative schools were highlighted within the past decade by researchers who identified the attributes of effective schools. Although the concept itself is not new, the suggestion that collaboration should become the norm for all schools is new.

Elements of the Collaborative School

As the many examples in these pages illustrate, there is no one model of the collaborative school. Collaboration describes a range of practices that can involve a handful of teachers or an entire faculty. Although collaboration can be encouraged by formal programs—organizational development, for instance—it cannot be imposed on a faculty or implemented as if it were a new reading series. Collaboration depends inherently on the voluntary effort of professional educators to improve their schools and their own skills through teamwork.

Because the collaborative school is a composite of beliefs and practices, it is easier to describe than to define. Perhaps the best way to characterize the collaborative school is to list its elements:

- The belief, based on effective schools research, that the quality of education is largely determined by what happens at the school site
- The conviction, also supported by research findings, that instruction is most effective in a school environment characterized by norms of collegiality and continuous improvement
- The belief that teachers are professionals who should be given responsibility for the instructional process and held accountable for its outcomes
- The use of a wide range of practices and structures that enable administrators and teachers to work together on school improvement
- The involvement of teachers in decisions about school goals and the means for achieving them.

Implicit in these elements is the overriding goal of the collaborative school: educational improvement. Although a host of other benefits may be expected to derive from collaboration—staff harmony, mutual respect between teachers and administrators, and a professional work environment for teachers—its primary rationale is the instructional effectiveness that results when teachers participate collegially in school improvement and their own professional growth. In support of this assertion, proponents of the collaborative school point to a growing body of research findings on the social and organizational context of teaching. These are reviewed in Chapter 2.

In terms of the roles of teachers, several distinguishing marks of collaborative schools are the "critical practices of adaptability" identified by Little (1982):

1. Teachers engage in frequent, continuous, and increasingly concrete and precise talk about teaching practice.

2. Teachers are frequently observed and provided with useful (if potentially frightening) critiques of their teaching.

3. Teachers plan, design, research, evaluate, and prepare teaching materials together.

4. Teachers teach each other the practices of teaching.

Chapters 2 and 3 provide numerous examples of these practices in action.

The collaborative school has much in common with the "school team" model of staff organization described by Finn (1985):

> An accumulating body of research about the characteristics of unusually effective schools indicates that schools in which children learn the most usually have a "collegial" staffing structure and a strong sense of common purpose among teachers and administrators. This is often described in the abstract as a "shared moral order" or a "school ethos," but what it comes down to is that the professional staff functions as a team: it has clear objectives, works together smoothly, shares goals that transcend those of individual members, and shares a sense of responsibility for the mutual enterprise.

Collaboration, then, is intended to facilitate instructional effectiveness. Toward this end, the collaborative relationships have both vertical and horizontal dimensions. That is, administrators cooperate with teachers and teachers cooperate with one another.

To many, the term *collaboration* brings to mind the idea of administrators sharing their authority with teachers and involving them in decisions. This is indeed an important focus of the collaborative approach to schooling. But its more important dynamic comes from teachers working together to improve their practice of teaching. It is the informally and formally structured interaction among teachers about instruction that distinguishes the collaborative school from earlier models of democratic management and participative decision making, even though it incorporates elements of these concepts.

The collaborative school also differs from traditional shared-governance concepts in its rationale for involving teachers. The traditional approach emphasizes the improved quality of decisions that results when management involves staff members in the decision process. In the collaborative school, teachers enjoy greater say because of their professional status. Principals draw on teachers' expertise in formulating school goals, and teachers are free, for the most part, to exercise their professional judgment in implementing those goals.

In sum, the collaborative school provides a climate and structure that encourage teachers as professionals to work together and with the principal and other administrators toward school improvement and professional growth.

What It Is Not

Some educators, while affirming the above characteristics as desirable for any school, may nonetheless respond negatively to the idea of collaboration. In anticipating objections that may be raised, it is useful to state what the collaborative school is *not*.

● **It does not seek discussion for its own sake.** Collaboration, some critics fear, means just a lot of talking that takes teachers away from their tasks. True, collegiality and participative decision making require a certain investment of time. But the involvement of teachers in decision making and the interaction of educators in their schools, while valuable in themselves, contribute to something of even greater value: quality education.

Research on the social and organizational environment of teaching has shown that the amount of interaction among teachers in itself bears no relationship to school effectiveness. It is the content of those interactions that determines their value. Rosenholtz (1989), for example, defines *collaboration* as "the extent to which teachers engage in help-related exchange." This definition focuses on the kinds of interactions believed to lead to improved teaching and learning.

When teachers trade stories about problem students, they may enjoy a sense of camaraderie. To be sure, teachers deserve to experience the satisfaction and congeniality that they derive even from this level of interaction. But when they also share teaching practices with one another or critique one another's teaching, they are engaging in activities that characterize successful schools.

● **It does not require school administrators to abdicate their authority.** Is the collaborative school a laissez faire approach to school management in which administrators hand over the reins of the school to teachers? This concern lies at the root of many objections to a collaborative approach.

We believe that strong leadership by the principal is essential to the success of any school. This is especially true of collaborative schools, whose leaders must overcome isolationism and direct their faculties in a cooperative effort for school improvement. Moreover, even though the principal involves teachers and others in important decisions about the school's direction, he or she retains final decision-making authority. Thus we affirm NEA and NASSP's (1986) definition of the *collaborative school* as "a school in which the professional autonomy of teachers and the managerial authority of principals are harmonized."

Although not abdicating their positions, principals must be willing to share authority for some matters traditionally assigned to them. Teachers will be empowered to take part in such tasks as setting school goals, allocating school resources, and overseeing their own professional development. Nevertheless, increased roles for teachers need not mean decreased authority for principals. Many principals of schools that have initiated collaborative practices have discovered that power shared is power gained: teachers' respect for them as leaders grew.

In this book, the emphasis of suggestions for restructuring schools is not so much on who governs but rather on finding new ways to marshall teachers' expertise for the purpose of improving schools.

- **It does not reduce teachers' accountability.** Some observers have expressed fear that teachers may misuse an increased sense of status by invoking "professionalism" to avoid doing what school administrators or the public want them to do. It is certainly possible that some teachers may adopt such a tactic.

To be sure, collaboration can be undermined by laziness, defensiveness, or indifference. Whatever structure is employed, a certain amount of pressure must be applied to overcome some individuals' resistance to change and growth. It is precisely here that the collaborative school enjoys a great advantage over the traditional school. Collaborative norms reinforce traditional methods of accountability by building consensus for school improvement. Individuals are more likely to respond to directives from administrators or legislative mandates if these actions are consistent with the expectations of their colleagues.

In the collaborative school, accountability is a collective activity. Teachers monitor one another's performance, set limits on one another's behavior, and assume responsibility for helping their colleagues to improve. These self-policing efforts are one of the truest measures of a faculty's professionalism.

The Scope of This Book

The focus of this book, then, is on collaboration as a strategy to improve the instructional effectiveness of a school's faculty. We hope that, as byproducts of this strategy, teachers will be accorded respect as professionals, administrators will sense that their efficacy grows, and all members of the school community will experience the satisfaction of accomplishing important goals through teamwork.

Before previewing the chapters, we should mention a few subjects not covered in these pages. For lack of space, we have had to forego discussing one of the more familiar practices that encourages collaboration: team teaching. For an excellent set of guidelines for developing teaching teams and other work groups in schools, see Snyder and Anderson (1986).

Logic as well as practical necessity dictates that if principals are to share power with teachers, then district officials must bestow proportionately increased responsibility and authority on principals. For example, a principal cannot give teachers control of a portion of the school budget unless the district office entrusts to the principal the discretionary use of certain funds. Readers interested in these issues are advised to consult "School-Based Management," a chapter in *School Leadership: Handbook for Excellence* (1989).*

This book does not deal with the involvement of parents and the community in the collaborative process. Again we acknowledge, as in

---

* *School Leadership: Handbook for Excellence* (second edition, 1989) is available from the ERIC Clearinghouse on Educational Management, 1787 Agate St., University of Oregon, Eugene 97403-5207.

the case of school-based management, compatibility between this topic and the principles of the collaborative school. But we must leave to others the task of charting a course for the involvement of people beyond the walls of the school.

In our opinion, reward-for-performance plans such as multiple salary schedules and merit pay are not a necessary part of the collaborative school. Despite their popularity with policy makers at the state and national levels, we have seen no evidence that such plans contribute to school quality or teacher effectiveness. Therefore, they do not enter into this book's discussion.

Also outside this book's scope is collaboration among principals, a promising concept inspired by the Harvard Principals' Center and similar centers around the country. Principals who learn from one another are more likely to emphasize collegiality among their faculties.

Here, then, is a brief look at what the book does contain: The benefits of collaboration are the subject of Chapter 2. Following a brief discussion of teacher isolation and its consequences, we discuss the positive effects of collaboration on school renewal, teacher satisfaction, teacher learning, cooperation among students, and school governance.

Chapter 3 is devoted to an extensive survey of structures and practices supportive of collaboration. We describe programs—many already implemented in schools—for involving teachers in school improvement efforts, in their own professional development, in peer review efforts, and in school decision making.

Finally, in Chapter 4, we recommend steps toward introducing collaboration in schools. These measures include the principal's role in advising teachers, supporting collegiality, and adopting a collaborative management style; the implementation of programs ranging from an organizational development strategy to faculty planning groups; and the practical considerations of time, finances, and training.

To keep this discussion on a concrete level, throughout the book we cite numerous examples of actual schools and teachers at work. We are especially indebted to six researchers—Lieberman and Miller (1984), Metz (1986), Ashton and Webb (1986), and Rosenholtz (1989)—whose case studies supplied many of the examples found in these pages.

In sum, this book examines the defects of the typical school structure, describes the educational benefits of the collaborative approach to schooling, outlines a variety of collaborative structures already in use in schools, and suggests ideas for introducing those structures in other schools that wish to become more collaborative.

To Principals and Others

The individual having the greatest influence on both the formal and the informal relationships among the adults in a school is the principal. Consequently, much of this book, including a large portion of the chapter on introducing collaboration in schools, is directed specifically to principals. We intend this to be more, however, than an administrators' guide to fostering collaborative work environments.

Building a collaborative school is inherently a group activity; no person acting alone, whatever his or her position of influence, can induce other adults in the school to function as a team unless they share the ideal of teamwork and commit their energy to making the ideal real.

Teachers are every bit as responsible for creating a collaborative environment as are principals. It is with this assumption that we address this book to the entire faculty and administration at each school, whom we hope will find in these pages inspiration and practical guidelines for their own collaborative efforts.

In selecting material for this book, we have also kept in mind the interests of district administrators, school board members, and educational policy makers at the state level. Many of the examples of collaborative practices cited in Chapter 3 are districtwide or statewide in scope, and Chapter 4 includes issues involved in the implementation of district- wide programs that encourage collaboration among educators at the school level.

Chapter 2

Are Collaborative Schools Effective Schools?

The argument for collaboration in schools is a straightforward one: If teachers and administrators view teaching as a collaborative endeavor, in which administrators work closely with teachers and teachers work closely with one another, then improved teaching and learning will result. In this chapter we consider the evidence in support of this assertion and paint a more detailed picture of collaborative schools in action. To appreciate the benefits of collaboration, it is useful first to review the consequences of the isolated conditions under which most teachers currently teach.

Isolation and Its Costs

One would expect that a profession dedicated to learning would be structured in such a way that its members could learn from one another. In this light, the isolation of teachers from other adults is a glaring anomaly. In most elementary schools teachers seldom have an opportunity to exchange more than a few pleasantries with their colleagues during the course of the working day. Even the lunchbreak—for most professionals a time to socialize with their coworkers—is for most elementary teachers a time to supervise children in the lunchroom or on the playground.

At the secondary level, teachers are allotted a preparation period and have other opportunities for more extensive contacts with one another. But when teachers do interact, they are more likely to talk about family matters, sports, and other outside interests than to share their expertise about teaching. This is not to say that teachers' social interactions are without value; as in all occupations, socializing builds camaraderie and helps to relieve the tensions of work. But if teachers interact only on a social level, they cannot contribute to one another's professional growth.

Limits on Growth

Lieberman and Miller (1984) observe that "it is perhaps the greatest irony—and the greatest tragedy of teaching—that so much is carried on in self-imposed and professionally sanctioned isolation." On *a priori* grounds alone, one is inclined to agree with their statement. If teachers perform their work in isolation, then no teacher can benefit from the help of others. Bird and Little (1986) state the problem succinctly:

> Teachers inherit the same images of teaching that we all do, struggle toward proficiency virtually alone, and accumulate as much skill and wisdom as they can by themselves. Superb teachers leave their marks on all of us. They leave no marks on teaching.

The isolated conditions under which teachers practice their profession impede professional growth by making it difficult for teachers to exchange ideas among themselves and with administrators. After studying teachers in 38 schools, Goodlad (1984) concluded, "The classroom cells in which teachers spend much of their time appear... symbolic of their relative isolation from one another and from sources of ideas beyond their own background experience."

In a study of teachers in Tucson, Ariz., Shedd (1985) observed that "the relative isolation of teachers—from administrators and, more especially, from each other—is one job feature that complicates and impedes teachers in the performance of their responsibilities."

Isolation compounds the problems that beginning teachers face as they embark on their profession. Drawing on his experience with very young teachers, Sarason (1982) concluded that they "are quite unprepared both for the loneliness of the classroom and the lack of relationships in which questions and problems can be asked and discussed without the fear that the teacher is being evaluated."

Isolation has serious consequences for the experienced teacher as well as for the novice. Rosenholtz (1985) regards isolation as "perhaps the greatest impediment to learning to teach or to improving existing skills" because it forces teachers to learn by trial and error. Where school structures and norms inhibit teachers from assisting one another, they must rely on "their own ability to detect problems and discern solutions." Cut off from exemplary role models, teachers "tend to fall back on models that they recall from their own student days," she says.

Professional Atrophy

The limits that teachers' isolation places on their professional growth explain in part, Rosenholtz suggests, why, in the case of teachers who have worked more than five years, there is little relationship between their years of experience and their effectiveness in the classroom.

> Teachers tend to reach their peak performance after about four or five years; thereafter, perhaps because of little new input, their effectiveness with students actually begins to decline.

In addition to the obvious waste involved when each teacher must learn the craft through his or her own experience, teacher isolation may contribute toward the tendency of teachers to resist changes suggested by educational reformers. Under the best of circumstances, change imposed from (or even suggested by) the outside can be viewed as threatening. And apprehensions about change are reinforced when one must face that change alone.

Origins of Isolation

Why is teacher isolation so prevalent? Several explanations have been offered. Lortie (1975), for example, focuses on the institutional characteristics of schools, such as their cellular organization. Others, believing that teachers themselves are responsible, point to teachers' defensiveness or lack of interpersonal skills.

Flinders (1988) found that the teachers he observed did actively strive to maintain their isolation from other adults, but he traces the reason for this self-imposed isolation to an effort to protect "the time and energy required to meet immediate instructional demands." Faced with around-the-clock task demands, the teachers simply lacked the time for collegial interactions. Their motive in isolating themselves was highly professional: "to provide the best instruction possible." Yet "paradoxically," Flinders notes, "the long-term effects of isolation undermine the very instructional quality that this work strategy is intended to protect."

It seems clear that whatever solutions to the problem of teacher isolation are proposed must deal with the instructional demands on teachers' time.

In contrast to the professional isolation that characterizes perhaps a majority of schools, faculty members in a growing number of schools give and accept advice, share ideas, and work together on school improvement projects. A detailed portrait of these collaborative schools emerges from recent studies by Ashton and Webb (1986) and by Rosenholtz (1989). The findings of these studies illustrate the actual practices that distinguish collaborative schools from other schools.

Portrait of a Collaborative School

As part of their study of the relationship between teachers' sense of efficacy and student achievement, Ashton and Webb examined two schools—a junior high school and a middle school. Although the primary focus of their work was not collaboration *per se*, their case studies do serve to highlight the differences between collaborative and noncollaborative practices.

The two schools that Ashton and Webb selected for their study were, in most respects, quite similar. Each enrolled between 900 and 1,000 sixth, seventh, and eighth graders. Each student body was composed of roughly one-third black students and two-thirds white students. In each school, roughly 45 percent of the students were entitled to free or reduced-price lunches. The principal difference between the two schools was in the way they were organized.

The junior high school was organized along traditional lines of grade level and subject specialization. Teachers' classrooms were grouped by subject area throughout the wings of the school. Teachers typically had little or no contact with their colleagues who taught other subjects to the same students.

In contrast, the middle school was organized on the basis of teachers having students in common. Each team of four or five teachers—specializing in different subject areas—worked with a group of 120 to

170 students. Members of a given team were assigned neighboring classrooms. Together they "coordinated their curriculum planning, designed lessons around common themes, diagnosed the learning problems of specific students, and made team decisions on how best to solve those problems."

Decision Making

At the middle school, policy decisions were generally made by a steering committee consisting of administrators, team leaders, and representatives from special areas such as physical education. On some issues, the principal might suggest that the committee consult with the individual teaching teams before arriving at decisions. On others, the committee might raise an issue, discuss possible solutions, and leave it up to the individual teams to do as they see fit. Here the middle school principal describes the manner in which individuals could become involved in the decision-making process (the brackets are Ashton and Webb's):

> On the individual level, anybody can come and speak to me or a team leader by themselves. But their next step is on the team basis [where] seven or eight teachers get together and talk about things. Often decisions are made on the team level. Then another step up is the Program Improvement Council, where team leaders or any individual can come with concerns. [Ideas] can be expressed there which have an umbrella effect [of spreading information] over the entire school. Administrators are a part of [the Council] too. So everyone hears the idea directly or indirectly.

In contrast to the decision-making process at the middle school, at the junior high, say Ashton and Webb, "the decision-making responsibility rested ambiguously with the principal and his administrative staff." The principal did discuss issues with his administrative staff and occasionally solicited opinions from individual teachers. Still, as one assistant principal put it, "Ted [the principal] says you're going to do that, and it gets done."

Professional Interactions Among Teachers

In their description of a typical day at the middle school, Ashton and Webb provide a capsule view of collaboration in action:

> Evidence of teamwork and community showed itself at the start of each day at the middle school. Before the first bell, faculty gathered in the teachers' lounge to sign in and check the mail for announcements. This gathering was an occasion for sharing news, anecdotes, and companionship, and for starting the day on a note of communal enthusiasm. During the day, teachers spent most of their time in their classrooms but, when the schedule allowed, they used the team planning room for parent conferences, meetings with students, coffee breaks, or formal and informal meetings with members of their own teams.

At the middle school, members of a teaching team typically found occasions to meet together informally as well as formally. As one teacher's comment makes clear, the focus of the informal meetings was generally the students:

> Lunch time is our big social time. As a matter of fact we even have special lunches. About once a month, we all bring in some things and eat together. We get a lot accomplished at lunch time talking about the kids. We don't necessarily sit there with the intention of talking about the kids but when you have just spent four hours with them, that's what you're thinking about. So that's what we talk about.

According to Ashton and Webb, teachers at the middle school felt united in their concern for the students, as illustrated by one teacher's comment:

> I just feel... there is no time here at school where we're not talking about something that'll benefit the kids in some way. It's not that we plan it that way; it just happens that way. That's where our concern is.

Another teacher said that the middle school's faculty used their teaching team as a resource in helping them to cope with students' problems (Ashton and Webb's brackets):

> If I become aware of a problem, it is very important for me to communicate with... my team about the student and the problem. On our team, we're constantly involved in the process of trying to help students. [Because we all teach] the same students [we can provide and get] lots of help.

In contrast to the teamwork in evidence at the middle school, teachers at the junior high school typically went their own way. Even when teachers were thrown together on formal committees, there was a tendency for teachers to divide the work according to their specialties, with each teacher doing his or her share alone. Ashton and Webb cite a member of a committee formed to prepare for an evaluation visit (their brackets):

> We started off meeting... together each day, each third period. And then things broke down so that.... Sally was doing some things with language and reading [with which] Francis and I weren't familiar [and] couldn't do. Francis was worrying with the Science Fair and the science curriculum. And then I started doing social studies. We sort of all branched off. It was just easier to go our separate ways.

According to Ashton and Webb, the junior high school offered "few opportunities to share ideas." Teachers seldom talked with one another, and when they did, the conversation was seldom related to the tasks of teaching. "Decision making did not necessitate faculty discussions because school decisions were made by administrators, and classroom decisions by individual teachers." Asked if the faculty members at the school shared a common philosophy, one teacher responded, "I don't know. I really don't know about that; I can't tell." When asked the same question, the principal replied that there were "40 teachers in the school and about as many different philosophies."

In sum, at the middle school, teachers and administrators viewed both teaching and governance as collegial activities (the principal had the last say in matters of school policy, but the teachers played a significant role). At the junior high school, both teachers and administrators considered teaching to be the job of teachers operating individually and policy making to be the job of administrators.

Ashton and Webb advise that their study of these two schools was not intended to show that one organization was better than the other; rather, it was intended to be a means of developing a tentative hypothesis regarding the relationship between a school's formal organization and the teachers' sense of efficacy. Similarly, our purpose in drawing from Ashton and Webb's study is not to claim that one method of formal organization promotes collaborative practices whereas the other does not.

Surely some schools organized along traditional lines qualify as collaborative schools, whereas some schools with faculties formally organized into teaching teams are conspicuously lacking in collaborative practices. Although a school's formal organization may indeed retard or encourage teachers to collaborate, other, perhaps more important factors shaping teachers' interactions are the school's leadership and the faculty's norms.

Teacher Relationships in Collaborative Schools

Another recent study casting light on collaborative practices and attitudes in schools is Rosenholtz's (1989) analysis of 78 schools in Tennessee. On the basis of questionnaires in which teachers described the extent to which the faculties at their schools engaged in collaborative practices, Rosenholtz separated the schools into three categories—13 collaborative schools, 15 isolated schools, and 50 temperately isolated schools (the schools that fell somewhere between isolated and collaborative).

Rosenholtz then interviewed 21 randomly selected teachers from 7 of the collaborative schools, 21 randomly selected teachers from 7 of the isolated schools, and 32 randomly selected teachers from 10 of the temperately isolated schools. She makes no mention of the school's formal organizational structures.

Sharing About Instruction

Rosenholtz found that when teachers in collaborative settings talked with one another, they usually shared instructionally related ideas and materials. For instance, one teacher said the faculty often talks about the instructional program, the curriculum, and students' progress. When teachers shared information about a particular student, it was usually for the purpose of finding ways to help the student learn more effectively. One teacher said the schools' faculty members discuss how to reward the highest achievers and how to help the lowest achievers.

In another collaborative setting, kindergarten teachers plan their activities together. For example, two teachers plan the week's math activities while two other teachers plan the reading activities. One teacher commented to Rosenholtz that it helps to pool ideas from several people instead of each having to plan their work alone.

In contrast, none of the teachers from isolated settings mentioned instructional planning as a form of sharing. When they shared information about students, the sharing usually took the form of swapping stories about a child's errant behavior or sympathizing with one another, rather than pooling resources to help the child.

In a 1985 article, Rosenholtz describes the ubiquitous and informal nature of teachers' sharing about their work:

> In collaborative settings, teachers interact whenever the opportunity arises—in training sessions, faculty meetings, hallways, teachers' lounges, and classrooms. This interaction stems from professional rather than social concerns and involves a greater number of faculty members than do the social conversations that typify less effective schools.

Perceptions of Teacher Leaders

Teachers from collaborative and isolated settings also differed markedly in describing their teacher leaders. Teachers from collaborative settings regarded as teacher leaders those who showed initiative and willingness to experiment with new ideas, who offered motivation to other teachers, and who were willing and able to help other teachers solve instructional problems. One teacher said that the leaders set a good example for how to work with children.

In contrast, teachers from isolated settings rarely equated teacher leadership with instructional endeavors. Instead, 61 percent of the respondents equated teacher leadership with union involvement or other activities not related to classroom instruction.

Helping Behaviors

Responses to one of the questions asked by Rosenholtz were particularly revealing in contrasting the attitudes of teachers from isolated settings with those of teachers from collaborative settings. She asked teachers what they do when they have a particularly difficult problem with a student.

Based on teachers' responses, Rosenholtz arrived at four conclusions. First, the more collaborative the school, the more likely the teachers were to seek help from students' parents, the principal, and other teachers.

Second, for teachers from isolated schools, student problems invariably meant behavior problems, whereas for teachers from collaborative schools, student problems also included academic ones.

Third, teachers from isolated schools tended to see students as the *source* of problems and hence saw punishment as the solution, whereas teachers from collaborative schools tended to see students as *having* problems and hence attempted to identify their source.

Rosenholtz's fourth conclusion is a corollary to the preceding one. Teachers from isolated schools tended to ask for help in punishing problem students (for example, sending the student to the principal to be paddled), whereas teachers from collaborative schools tended to seek outside expertise to help the students solve their problems (for example, asking the student's parents about factors in the students' home life that might affect his or her performance).

"In collaborative schools," Rosenholtz wrote in her 1985 article, "teachers increasingly come to believe that student learning is possible with even the most difficult students and that they have access to the knowledge and skills to reach such students."

In summary, Rosenholtz's findings paint a clear picture of what distinguishes the school with collaborative norms from schools in which norms of isolation prevail. In collaborative schools, teachers plan instruction together and share ideas, they identify teacher leaders as those teachers who promote improved instructional practices, and they do not hesitate to seek help from other teachers, the principal, and parents when faced with children they consider to have problems.

On the face of it, all these activities would seem to lead to improved teaching and learning. But does empirical evidence exist showing that students actually perform better in schools with norms of collaboration than they do in schools with norms of isolation?

We now turn to that question.

Benefits of Collaboration

Rosenholtz (1989) may have been the first researcher to attempt a large-scale statistical analysis of the relationship between teacher collaboration and student achievement. Quantitative data gathered from her statewide representative sample of 78 elementary schools in eight school districts show that collaboration is a strong predictor of student achievement gains in reading and math. The gains were measured with one cohort of students from second through fourth grades. A regression analysis controlled for school socioeconomic status, school size, teacher experience, teachers' verbal ability, and pupil-teacher ratio.

Several case studies and the results of the effective schools research also suggest a correspondence between collaborative norms and improved teaching and learning.

Little (1982) conducted case studies of four schools identified as successful on the basis of student achievement on standardized achievement scores and two schools identified as unsuccessful on the basis of the same criteria. She found that the successful schools were characterized by frequent teacher evaluations and feedback on them, teachers talking with one another about teaching, teachers working together to design their classes, and teachers teaching each other about teaching. All these collaborative practices were conspicuously absent in the unsuccessful schools.

From their review of research on effective schools, Purkey and Smith (1983) identified four process variables that "define the general concept of school culture and climate": collaborative planning and collegial relationships, sense of community, clear goals and high expectations commonly shared, and order and discipline. Concerning the first of these variables, they say:

> Collegiality serves many purposes. Chief among them are that it breaks down barriers between departments and among teachers/administrators, encourages the kind of intellectual sharing that can lead to consensus, and promotes feelings of unity and commonality among the staff.

In another discussion of effective schools research, Bacharach and others (1984) noted that effective schools paid particular attention to the following processes:

> (1) goal-setting, in which goals and objectives for the school as a whole are generated and revised; (2) close monitoring and evaluation of programs, curricula, individual student progress, and individual teacher performance, through informal as well as formal procedures; and (3) staff development, not confined to formal training sessions, but pursued through day-to-day exchanges of information between teachers and administrators and among teachers themselves.

Bacharach and his associates add that *"whatever changes are made in the management of our schools should be the product of cooperative agreement and mutual problem solving.* Changes that one party must impose on others are, almost by definition, changes that will undermine the effectiveness of our schools" (their emphasis).

In Rutter and others' (1979) longitudinal analysis of performance by a group of students in London's inner city schools, the more successful schools were characterized by intellectual sharing, collaborative planning, and collegial work among the teachers.

Teachers' Professional Development

We have already cited Rosenholtz (1989) in describing the attitudes and practices prevalent in collaborative schools. In the same study, Rosenholtz analyzed the effect of collaborative norms on teachers' perception of teacher learning.

Rosenholtz found that teachers felt they continued to learn about their profession throughout their careers where the following conditions existed: schools set clearly defined goals for teaching improvement, principals used teacher evaluations as tools to help teachers improve, principals and faculties shared values about teaching, and collaboration between principals and faculties and among faculty members was the norm. Conversely, where these conditions did not prevail, teachers tended to believe that they had learned all they need to know about teaching within the first few years after entering the profession.

Collaborative settings are particularly beneficial for beginning teachers, as Rosenholtz (1985) explains:

> There is less reason for novices to cover their mistakes and hide their inadequacies in collaborative settings than in isolated ones. Indeed, there are compelling reasons to disclose one's early mistakes. For example, the cohesiveness of the faculty impels beginners to become involved in professional discussions. Then, too, novices maximize their own intrinsic rewards when they seek the advice and assistance of others, because better teaching is the result.

To the degree that successful staff development programs and continuous teacher learning have an effect on student achievement, these studies would support the proposition that norms of collaboration contribute to improved teaching and learning. As Barth (1986) points out,

"No profession can survive, let alone flourish, when its members are cut off from others and from the rich knowledge base on which success and excellence depend."

Student Cooperation

When teachers do work together, their example encourages students to do the same, as Schmuck and Schmuck (forthcoming) explain:

> Teachers who practice communication skills (learned through their involvement in an organizational development project) with one another also tend to use similar communication skills with their students in the classroom. Also, teachers who are comfortable cooperating with one another tend to feel comfortable asking their students to cooperate in the classroom. They view the school as a community of humans engaged in cooperative learning and cooperative development. They believe that power should be shared by all, including the students, and that, whenever possible, decisions should be made by those who will be affected by the decision.

In short, the Schmucks state, a collaborative school climate "sets the stage, facilitates, and makes possible student cooperation in the classroom."

An example substantiating the Schmucks' claim is found in Metz's study (1986) of the Heartland School District (a fictitious name she gave to a district she studied). At the district's Adams Avenue School for Individually Guided Education, teams of four teachers each worked with blocks of students. Within each classroom, students were grouped according to skill level, and the members of each group worked together at a table. Such arrangements encouraged cooperation among teachers and encouraged students to work together. The program at Jesse Owens Open Education School, while differing in many details, placed similar emphasis on cooperative teaching and learning.

In contrast, the Horace Mann School for the Gifted and Talented offered nothing special in the way of goals or teaching technologies. Each teacher basically did what he or she had always done before, meaning, in practice, a heavy emphasis on lecture, recitation, and seatwork. Teachers generally moved all students through the same curriculum at the same pace; some would find the work too easy and become bored, whereas others would be forced to strain to avoid falling by the wayside.

Metz notes that interracial cooperation in the classroom and interracial friendships among the students were both more common at Jesse Owens and Adams Avenue than they were at Horace Mann. At the same time, she points out, much more racial tension was evident at Horace Mann than at the other two schools.

Collegial Management Styles

The merits of participative management—one component of the collaborative school—are the subject of a body of literature too large to be reviewed here. In lieu of such a review, Bebermeyer (1982) characterizes well the collaborative style of effective instructional leaders:

What is it that the leader initiates? On closer examination of the indicators of effective leaders, one is attracted to the conclusion that the leader initiates *cooperation*. How? By cooperating—by initiating practices and processes that take into account the desires and dignity of others, whether by shared decision making, open communication, participative problem solving or other ways. The leader initiates cooperation not only by personal example but also by establishing and encouraging cooperative structures, whether that means collegial teams in inservice activities or teaching or learning teams in classrooms.

In sum, with the help of studies reviewed in this chapter, we have seen numerous examples of teachers engaging in collaborative practices: talking about teaching practices, observing one another teach, planning and preparing teaching materials together, and teaching one another the practices of teaching. Do collaborative practices such as these lead to improved teaching and learning? To date few studies have examined this issue directly. But Rosenholtz's data, research on effective schools, and several studies of school improvement efforts point to a strong association between collaborative norms/practices and student achievement, school renewal, and teachers' openness to learning. Moreover, schools whose teachers cooperate with one another are characterized by cooperation among students.

Given the problems associated with past efforts at educational reform that have *not* focused on interactions among teachers at the school site, a strong case can be made that the fostering of collaborative norms and practices within the school well deserves attention by educators.

If we are convinced that collaboration should be cultivated, our next task is to identify structures that encourage teachers and administrators to work together.

Chapter **3**

A Survey
of Collaborative
Practices

Two primary defects of many schools are a structure and accompanying set of social norms that isolate teachers from one another and a bureaucratic management style that alienates teachers from administrators. Teachers cannot be expected to adopt new patterns of interacting with colleagues, and administrators cannot be expected to share their power with teachers, unless new, more effective structures can be created.

Do better ways of organizing the school's work environment exist? And if so, do they work? This chapter surveys a variety of alternative practices and structures, most of them already implemented in schools, that command positive answers to both these questions. Schools that have gained experience with collaboration can now serve as models for other schools.

Those who propose these practices leave no doubt that changes are mandatory if public education is to improve. "To put it bluntly," say Ward and her colleagues (1985) at the Northwest Regional Educational Laboratory, "what we know about quality schools, about the characteristics of effective organizations, about the forthcoming replacement of teachers, and about the professionalization of teaching demands that such steps be taken. A school district that opts not to move in this direction will most likely make a major error."

Rosenholtz (1989) points out that the school's organizational conditions function either as a centripetal force pulling teachers to pursue common purpose or as a centrifugal force pushing teachers to pursue individual purpose. A major benefit of the practices described here is that they enable teachers to work as a team. They make each school a community where the faculty works together on such common goals as school improvement and professional growth.

The following sections review methods for involving teachers in school improvement efforts, in their own professional development, in peer review programs, and in decisions about the school's instructional program. Finally, we outline some implications of these collaborative practices for teachers and administrators.

School Improvement as a Communal Responsibility

According to the Carnegie Task Force on Teaching as a Profession, teachers are "the primary source of expertise for improving schools." Opportunities for involving teachers in school improvement are plentiful.

> As the weight of the current bureaucratic environment is lifted and support staff take over many non-instructional tasks, professional teachers can concentrate on inspiring, coaching, guiding, and motivating students, and applying other resources, including technology, to the task of improving student learning. Teachers can help each other analyze student problems, work with parents, help students master particularly tough concepts, develop materials and curricula, organize the work of the support staff, hire new staff and decide how to allocate the budget among competing claims. Such schools will provide a greatly improved environment for teaching.

Lead Teachers

The initiative for these school improvement efforts would come, proposed the task force, from a group of lead teachers in each school. These experienced teachers would guide and influence the activity of others, ensuring that the skill and energy of their colleagues are drawn on as the organization improves its performance. The task force realized that collegial relationships in a school's faculty do not just automatically happen. Someone must initiate efforts to create communities, to get teachers to work together. Although lead teachers can perform this function, so, too, can principals.

Lead teachers play a critical role in the instructional improvement efforts of a consortium of Oregon school districts. The Valley Education Consortium (VEC), as described by Fielding and Schalock (1985), is an organization of school districts, education service districts, a state-supported educational research and development agency, and a state college. The consortium follows a model of school improvement that emphasizes the importance of developing and field testing instructional programs, systematically evaluating program costs and benefits, and using evaluation results to guide improvements.

The Valley Education Consortium involves lead teachers in developing the instructional programs.

> Many of the VEC lead teachers have been involved for five or six years in building and refining curriculum, test items, and other assessment procedures contained in VEC programs. They have done this both during the school year with released time furnished by their districts and during the summer. Lead teachers not only have drafted products, but have modified and extended them in view of critiques from both peers and experts in the field. They have gained invaluable insights about the nature of goal-based programs through this demanding development work.

Working with principals, lead teachers introduce the new programs to the remainder of the staff and help their colleagues to implement the programs. They also assist in monitoring program implementation by administering questionnaires to their colleagues on the level of use of

VEC programs. To prepare the lead teachers for their role of assisting their colleagues, school districts in the consortium provide released time for lead teachers to attend a seminar that meets periodically throughout the school year.

School Improvement Teams

Taking root in several schools across the country are innovative models of school improvement that induce teachers and administrators to work together as teams. In some of these instances the personnel at each school site developed the program on their own, and in other cases the school teams are part of larger networks for renewing schools.

Individual-Site Models. In a catalog of new roles for teachers, Ward and her colleagues (1985) cite examples of improvement teams that capitalize on the leadership provided by teachers. A school improvement team in an elementary school, for example, consists of the school principal and four to six teachers. At a high school a leadership team consisting of the principal, counselors, representative teachers, and other school staff members keeps track of the school as a whole.

This and other team improvement efforts in this school "have eliminated the need for department heads or assistant principals," say the authors. Teachers in this school also work with the principal to develop the school's annual budget and to hire new staff.

Mastery in Learning Project. A promising team approach for improving teaching, learning, and the curriculum is the National Education Association's Mastery in Learning Project, launched in 1985. From a pilot test in six schools during the 1985-86 school year, the project spread to 24 schools that formed a national network of demonstration sites. School officials at each site have empowered teachers to create the necessary conditions for mastery to be achieved.

The Mastery in Learning Project specifies three major activities that the faculty at each school carry out. First, the faculty prepares a detailed description of the school, including demographic data and indicators of student attitudes and performance. Next, the faculty members divide into groups to work on issues and problems identified through the inventory process, say Lee and Obermeyer (1986). Much time is devoted to gathering research findings on such topics as critical thinking, writing skills, and developmental curriculum.

Finally, the faculty members develop, test, and implement a school improvement action plan. At the pilot schools the testing phase will continue until 1989, when the plans will be ready for implementation. At one school, for example, a committee is using control groups to test approaches to teaching critical thinking.

Lee and Obermeyer report that at least half the staff members at the pilot sites are actively involved in the project. "Time for teachers to engage in the project is drawn from days reserved by the school system for staff development, from a time bank established for the project, and from time volunteered by individuals."

Mathematics Cooperatives. Encouraging teachers to work for school improvement is one goal of the Urban Mathematics Collaborative, an effort by the Ford Foundation to improve the teaching of mathematics in inner city schools. According to Nelson (1987), the mathematics collaboratives—installed in 11 cities—focus the energies of high school math teachers on projects to improve their profession. For example, in Pittsburgh and Cleveland, says Nelson, teachers "are pilot teaching textbooks and studying their comparative effectiveness." Teachers in these cities also review materials of their own making for inclusion in mathematics teachers' resource centers.

Nelson points out that the collaboratives are dealing with some of the deeper structural problems of teaching that derive from outmoded, turn-of-the-century models of teaching, learning, and schooling. For instance, the efforts of principals, mathematics supervisors, and superintendents to trust and share power with teachers are helping to overcome institutional divisiveness. Moreover, teachers view the collaboratives as a welcome relief from their typical isolation; they "are aching simply to talk with each other, to watch each other teach, to enrich the web of social and professional interaction that supports each mathematics classroom," Nelson says.

> The larger issue here is the degree to which, in general, teaching has been conceived of as an activity that is narrowly instrumental and improvable by specific technical fixes, rather than an activity that is open-ended, rich in ideas and relationships, and conducted by people who think broadly and creatively about their subject and the learning and teaching of it.

National Network for Educational Renewal. Goodlad believes that individual schools must have outside support if they are to succeed in renewing themselves. In an interview by Olson (1987), Goodlad explains the pitfalls of go-it-alone approaches:

> For one institution to renew itself is very difficult and very dangerous, because if you do anything significant, you'll be shot down. It's the rate-buster syndrome. The person who goes on the assembly line and thinks he can do 16 pieces an hour instead of 12 gets beat up.

Providing support for schools that want to change is the rationale for Goodlad's National Network for Educational Renewal, which consists of 14 partnerships between 17 universities and about 100 school districts. In addition to the help that will come from the universities, schools in the partnerships can also rely on the support of their districts' superintendents, who are members of the partnerships' governing bodies.

Although the partnerships will seek to address a broad set of goals, such as improving the preparation of teachers and heightening equal access to schooling, a major focus will be "a redistribution of power among teachers, professors, principals, and school superintendents," Olson reports. School improvement teams are one important strategy for replacing the traditional top-down decision-making structure with a more decentralized system.

For example, in the Southern Maine Partnership, says Olson, "four groups of teachers are now meeting monthly on problems specific to early childhood education, mathematics, middle schools, and high schools." Each school in the Massachusetts Coalition for School Improvement has an improvement team that consists of the principal and four to six teachers. "The team members are supposed to work together to identify improvements in the curriculum, instruction, and other school conditions that would enhance student learning."

In sum, a common assumption of all the models reviewed in this section is that profound and lasting change at the level of the school site must be the product of self-renewal on the part of the personnel at the site, rather than the product of mandates imposed from above.

Program Evaluation by Teachers

At an elementary school highlighted by Ward and her colleagues (1985), teachers play a major role in evaluating the education program of the school. Each year the teachers establish objectives for improvement and then take steps to implement them. To make sure the improvements will be made, the teachers use standardized and criterion-referenced test data (supplied by the district office) to monitor their students' academic achievement. For example, when a new social studies program was adopted, the teachers wanted to know whether students acquired the new skills that the materials and strategies were to produce. The assistant superintendent's office analyzes the achievement data and provides the teachers with special reports that answer such questions.

Cooperative Professional Development

One of the chief characteristics of a profession is that its members assume responsibility for their professional development. In the collaborative school, teachers participate collegially in their professional growth. When the professionals in such a school design their development program, they may choose among a diverse set of models. Among the different types of programs that involve teachers in mutual efforts to improve their professional skills are peer observation, peer coaching, teacher centers in which expert teachers train other teachers, mentor teacher programs, and teacher support teams.

Peer Observation

Research on effective schools has stressed the importance of regular observation of teachers' classroom performance. Teachers improve when they are observed and given feedback by someone who can identify and reinforce the teachers' strengths, discern their weaknesses, and assist them in carrying out an improvement strategy. Teachers can also learn from observing other teachers model their effective teaching. Little and Bird (1984) state that "observing and being observed, giving and getting feedback about one's work in the classroom, may be among the most powerful tools of improvement."

Although observation of teachers' classroom performance is traditionally handled by principals, time constraints and the problem of trust (principals decide whether teachers will be retained, promoted, and given tenure) prevent many principals from carrying out this role effectively.

Brophy (1979) suggests that, although any observer can provide feedback, peer observation seems to work best. "Working as a group," says Brophy, "teachers not only get useful feedback relevant to their individual interests, but begin to work together, sharing expertise and observations and breaking down the isolation that so often is a barrier to professional development."

Peer observation has been used intermittently in a small number of schools for many years. Although the results have been mostly encouraging, various obstacles—chief among them the isolation and fragmentation fostered by the traditional school structure—have prevented the widespread implementation of this professional development model.

Today's renewal of interest in peer observation is a by-product of the movement to professionalize teaching. Peer review is acknowledged to be the hallmark of a profession, whose practitioners monitor one another's performance. In fact, peer review is so essential to the reform of the teaching profession that it provides the best argument for renewing the school's structure. Whereas peer observation once was declared unworkable because it was at odds with the typical school's isolation of teachers and hierarchical authority structure, now reformers argue it is necessary to reshape the school's culture and structure to create a supportive environment for peer observation.

One model of collegial observation, advocated by Glatthorn (1984) for "competent, experienced teachers," has the following features:

1. The relationship is moderately formalized and institutionalized. It is not simply an informal exchange of an occasional visit by two or more teachers who are close associates.

2. At a minimum the teachers agree to observe each other's classes at least twice and to hold conferences after those visits.

3. The relationship is among peers. Although an administrator or supervisor may be involved in organizing and occasionally monitoring the program, the observations, conferences, and discussions involve only teachers.

4. The relationship is nonevaluative. It is intended to complement, not take the place of, standard evaluation systems. None of the observation or conference data are shared with administrators or made part of the evaluation process.

(Peer review programs that supplement or actually replace traditional evaluation systems are described in the following section.)

Calling this program of peer observation "cooperative professional development," Glatthorn points out that it can take many forms, "from modest programs of two or three exchanges of observations to very ambitious and comprehensive projects in which teams of teachers collaborate in several aspects of the instructional function."

A program that shares the four features recommended by Glatthorn is the Stanford Collegial Evaluation Program, developed by sociologist Sanford Dornbusch and his associates at Stanford University's Center for Research and Development in Teaching in the mid-seventies. Drawing from results of field tests to highlight those practices that were most effective, Roper and Hoffman (1986), members of Dornbusch's team, describe the program's operation.

The authors are quick to point out that the program involves formative, not summative, evaluation; the program's purpose is "to improve instruction, not to gather evidence of improper performance for disciplinary action." The data—gathered from collegial observations, student questionnaires, and self-assessments—are used only for professional development purposes.

The Stanford Collegial Evaluation Program links teachers in reciprocal team relationships so that participants take turns observing each other. This reciprocal arrangement means that teachers are not thrust into a supervisory role, say Roper and Hoffman. The program is also flexible in that any number of teachers in a school can participate.

Teachers carry out seven interdependent steps: choosing a partner, selecting criteria, self-assessment, evaluation by students, observation, conferences, and planning a program of improvement. The entire sequence requires 10 to 12 hours spread over a month or two.

Field tests revealed several barriers to successful implementation of collegial observation, as well as strategies for overcoming those barriers.* For example, teachers who are fearful need to be assured that the program is voluntary, confidential, and solely for their own professional growth. Another problem—the low validity and reliability of observations by untrained peers—unfortunately applies to teacher evaluations in general, whether the observer is the principal or a peer.

Teachers' reluctance to offer constructive criticism stood out prominently in the field tests. But candor may grow with experience in the program: "It takes time to break the norm of never criticizing (constructively or otherwise) one's colleagues," say Roper and Hoffman. Another problem—that of finding time in a busy school schedule for teachers to observe one another—is actually a problem of priorities, the authors believe. "Convincing the powers that be that teachers are professionals who learn best from one another is the central issue," they say.

Roper and Hoffman state that an especially difficult obstacle is an unsupportive school context—one "hostile to the values of pro-

---

*Directions and forms for implementing the Stanford Collegial Evaluation Program, along with examples of successful practices, are available in a manual. The Field Test Edition of *The Collegial Evaluation Program: A Manual for the Professional Development of Teachers,* by Sanford M. Dornbusch, Terrence E. Deal, Deborah Plumley, and Susan S. Roper, was published in 1976 by the Stanford Center for Research and Development in Teaching, Stanford University. Copies, at $10.00 each, can be ordered from the Oregon School Study Council, 1787 Agate St., University of Oregon, Eugene 97403. Quantity discounts are available.

fessionalism, individualization, and collegiality." Peer observation requires a school context marked by norms of experimentation, mutual encouragement, and collective effort toward school improvement. The principal's role in fostering such norms in a school is discussed in the following chapter.

Peer Coaching

One way to improve teachers' instructional effectiveness is to provide them with encouragement and technical assistance as they attempt to apply new knowledge and skills. This process, known as "coaching," has been studied by Showers (1984) and her colleagues at the University of Oregon. "There seems little doubt," says Showers, "that teachers can be trained to coach their peers in a school environment."

Fielding and Schalock (1985) summarize Showers' research as follows: Six peer coaches received 18 hours of training to increase their understanding of designated instructional models and ways they might be applied and adapted. These 6 teachers were also trained in the process of coaching. They then coached 15 other teachers, observing and conferring with them weekly. In addition to supporting and encouraging the trainees, the coaches also gave technical advice, helped their trainees determine where a model might best be applied, and adapted the models to fit the characteristics of particular students.

According to Fielding and Schalock, the coaches "carried out their roles effectively and coached teachers used the new instructional models more skillfully and in more appropriate areas of learning than did partially coached or uncoached teachers."

Coaching benefits not only the trainees but the coaches themselves, a finding that led Showers to suggest that all teachers should be peer coaches. She found that all the peer coaches in her study were regarded by their trainees as helpful and professional in their conduct, regardless of the teachers' previous friendship patterns. Although several coaches expressed concern about being in a role that made them appear to be "superior" to their peers, they successfully overcame these anxieties.

Showers notes that teachers and administrators must be creative in organizing peer coaching systems to free up teachers' time:

> In schools where teachers already have preparation periods scheduled into their work days, teachers can be organized into coaching teams for collaborative planning and feedback sessions. Some schools have used specialist teachers to release teachers for observation periods, and some principals have taken classes in order to provide observation times for teachers. In other cases, teachers have had to videotape lessons for sharing at a later time when live observations could not be arranged. In the peer coaching study reported here, substitutes were provided for peer coaches one day per week in order for them to complete their observations and conferences.

All these strategies require the active support and involvement of principals, she points out.

Neubert and Bratton (1987) report the implementation of a model they call *team coaching:* Instead of observing teachers, the coaches worked alongside the teachers in planning, executing, and evaluating the lessons. Team coaches had flexible schedules so they could visit each teacher's classroom twice a week.

A teacher interviewed by Neubert and Bratton comments about her experience with this model:

> I don't have time to share ideas with other teachers and, even if I did, I'm not sure it would work quite as well. My coach takes time to plan with me, schedule herself into my classroom, and also debrief at the end of the lesson. We've gotten it down to 45 minutes on Tuesdays and Thursdays. It works, but I could easily use her every day.

The peer coaches in Showers' study regarded their access to a consultant, through weekly staff meetings, as essential for their success. For this reason she recommends that districts provide some means of ongoing support and training for peer coaches. This training should focus on both the content they are seeking to share with their peers and on the process of coaching.

Teaching Clinic with Expert Teachers

In an address to a fall 1985 Conference of the Council of the Great City Schools, Edward J. Meade, Jr., chief program officer of the Ford Foundation, argued that school officials must go beyond merely assigning responsibility for professional development to teachers. It will not help matters to give teachers responsibility for their own development but deny them the time and resources to carry it out. Whether a program encompasses an entire district or a single school, it is the responsibility of school authorities, said Meade, to create the context—structure, time, and resources—for teacher development to take place.

Pointing out that hospitals require doctors to attend seminars on hospital time, and that corporations provide and often mandate education and training on the job for their executives, Meade argued that teachers should be allowed to carry out their development on company time. New structures must be created so that teacher development can take place on the job as a regular ongoing activity of a school.

As an example of such structures, Meade pointed to Pittsburgh's Schenley High School Teacher Center, a citywide teacher development program that is akin to teaching hospitals in the medical world. In this school, "able and knowledgeable practitioners are engaged in guiding and assisting other practitioners to improve the practice of their particular craft."

Lawrence E. Davis (1986), associate director of staff development for the Pittsburgh Public Schools, explains that the teaching clinic at Schenley was designed to give all teachers in the district's secondary schools a periodic professional development experience. The center operates as a regular school but has a staff that includes a specially trained clinic coordinator and two clinical resident teachers who have received extensive training in effective teaching. Recipients of the training are four visiting teachers, who have been released from their regular assignments throughout the district to attend the clinic.

Ward and her colleagues (1985), who also highlight this creative program in the Pittsburgh Public Schools, note that the clinical resident teachers teach students for approximately three hours a day and devote the remainder of the time to conducting model lessons and to planning with, observing, and coaching the center's visiting teachers.

Visiting teachers cycle in and out of the clinic at eight-week intervals. While at the clinic they participate in an intense process of peer observation. Under the leadership of the resident teachers, visiting teachers as a group observe one another's teaching and collaboratively analyze the data before giving feedback. In addition, each visiting teacher is coached by a resident teacher. "This one to one dialogue complements the skills and understandings nurtured in the teaching clinic," says Davis.

The visiting teachers at Schenley also receive about 30 hours of training in effective teaching. Designed to promote collegial relationships and dialog, the training takes a variety of forms, as Davis notes:

> Daily professional seminars, peer conferences, externships, common workspaces, committee work, scheduled common preparation times and clinics all provide visiting teachers with opportunities for professional interaction.

Upon leaving the clinic, visiting teachers often state that they valued most the opportunity for professional interaction with their peers, and many of them go on to initiate peer observations and feedback at their home schools. Principals in the district support these efforts, says Davis, with creative scheduling, collaborative teacher projects, instructional cabinets, peer observation activities, and teacher seminars.

A similar program being planned by the Jefferson County Public Schools in Louisville, Ky., goes under the name of "professional-development schools." According to Olson (1986), these schools "will provide the clinical settings for educators to assimilate the values, norms, and practices associated with effective teaching while receiving close supervision and support." Of the county's approximately 145 public schools, 24 have applied to become planning sites for the new professional-development schools.

Teacher Institutes

One way in which teachers can initiate and sustain their own improvement efforts is through a teacher institute. Lieberman and Miller (1984) describe an institute administered by an English teacher released half time from classroom duties. That teacher, in turn, uses teachers from throughout the district to conduct workshops on subjects of interest to teachers, rather than subjects chosen by the district's central office.

Because the head of the institute is chosen by the local teachers' organization, the teachers' own organization is in charge and held accountable for teachers' professional development. And, because the individuals conducting the workshops are practicing teachers and the content of the workshops is not theoretical but tried in the classroom, workshop leaders are respected.

Mentor Programs

Mentor programs can stimulate collaboration among faculty members to the degree they involve mentors in coaching other teachers and facilitating their professional development. An example of a teacher mentor program is the Charlotte-Mecklenburg (N.C.) School District's Teacher Career Development Program. This program, state Ward and colleagues (1985), is founded on the premise that a teacher with 20 years of experience and advanced training is capable of performing more complex and different roles than a new teacher.

Teachers in this district advance through three stages: provisional, career nominee, and career. Teachers at the last stage who qualify on several criteria may apply to be senior teacher mentors. Charged with coaching and advising provisional teachers, mentor teachers also serve on an advisory/assessment team that conducts the formative and summative assessments of the provisional teacher's classroom performance.

Meade (1985) draws several conclusions about effective teacher mentor programs from the findings of a report on teacher development in schools recently prepared for the Ford Foundation by the Academy for Educational Development. Common to the different kinds of mentor teachers described in the academy's report are these features:

- The mentor is a peer of other teachers (we know from research that professionals of all kinds learn much of what they learn from peers).
- The mentor continues to teach (stays immersed in the "real" school world).
- The mentor has a special responsibility that he or she must use to help others.
- The mentor has the time and resources to carry out this assignment on the job.

Programs such as these that create different categories of roles for teachers are to be preferred, says Meade, over master teacher schemes that create a hierarchy of teachers.

Voicing a similar preference, Freiberg (1984-85) points out that "the hierarchical nature of proposed master teacher programs focuses on individual advancement rather than improving the quality of the learning environment throughout the school."

As Rosenholtz (1987) points out, "a career ladder system will help teachers improve only if it increases collaboration."

Mentor programs provide an ideal focus for interdistrict cooperation, according to the experience of three school districts near Albany, N.Y. Warner (1987), a mentor teacher for the Greater Capital Region Teacher Center, reports that veteran teachers appreciated having a mentor who was sent by a district other than the one in which they taught. "Relationships were fresh, communications were open, development was stimulated, and perspectives were broadened."

Also, the mentor's neutrality lowered everyone's risks. The sharing of mentors across district boundaries would not meet beginning teachers' needs, however, because their mentors must be able to explain the procedures and policies unique to the new teachers' own schools and districts.

When planning a mentor teacher program, a district will want to determine the most pressing needs of its schools (the Charlotte-Mecklenburg program, for example, focuses on coaching beginning teachers). Hence, if a state government decides to make funds available for mentor programs, it should allow school districts wide latitude in designing their programs.

The California Mentor Teacher Program offers a good example. According to Wagner (1986), "Legislative requirements are minimal and local discretion enormous, as most of the candidate qualifications, mentoring duties, and support functions are locally defined."

Allowing such discretion enables each school district to do what Charlotte-Mecklenburg did—analyze its own needs and develop the program best suited to satisfying those needs.

Teacher Support Team

Another model for collegial professional development is the teacher support team, described by Sgan and Clark (1986) as a school-based cadre of professionals who provide systematic support and assistance to individual teachers.

These teams provide both one-on-one and group support, depending on the needs of the teacher receiving help. Sgan and Clark list the following activities that support teams can engage in:

- Assessing teachers and programs
- Observing teachers
- Meeting with teachers
- Providing feedback on teacher performance and program effectiveness
- Conducting instructional planning sessions with teachers
- Developing and selecting materials and resources
- Helping to implement new ideas
- Initiating teacher and program improvement.

"It is imperative that the principal be a member of the support team," say Sgan and Clark, so that the team will be sanctioned "as a legitimate structure for teacher supervision and support in the school." The team should also include a mentor teacher or someone of similar position, such as a department head. One or two other teachers, selected by peers, round out the team.

The principal coordinates the team by arranging its meetings and providing released time for members, but classroom teachers must be the major decision-making group.

Reflective Casebooks

"If collegiality is defined," says Shulman (1989), "as that set of strategies needed to overcome the limitations of individual rationality and to make learning from experience possible," then it includes both face-to-face interactions and the sharing of knowledge among colleagues at remote sites through publications, correspondence, and the like. As one way to achieve this kind of "invisible" collegiality, Shulman encourages teachers to write "cases and casebook of teaching," in which they share with colleagues what they have learned from experience.

> The writing of cases serves as an occasion for reflection and deliberation on teaching by the case authors themselves. The cases, when written and distributed, can elicit commentaries by other teachers as well as by education scholars and teacher educators. These case-based exchanges can well create an entirely new form of educational discourse that centers on the experiences, reflections, and lessons learned by teachers.

Recently published collections of cases written by mentor teachers and intern teachers serve as a model for teachers who wish to explore this innovative professional development opportunity.*

Evaluation of Teachers as Professionals

For years educators have looked for alternatives to traditional teacher evaluation practices, which are faulted for being both ineffective and injurious to teachers' self-respect. Evaluation strategies that rely on standardized checklists and other bureaucratic methods continue to be widely used even though they contribute little to teacher growth.

As Rand Corporation researchers Wise and Darling-Hammond (1984-85) put it, "Bureaucratic evaluation may be sufficient for monitoring whether the teacher is performing in a minimally adequate fashion, but it typically cannot assess higher levels of competence or deliver valued rewards or advice to most teachers."

Further, in imposing bureaucratic procedures and expectations on professionals, traditional evaluation practices demoralize teachers.

Characteristics of Professional Evaluation

In the search for alternatives, educators and researchers have re-assessed both how evaluations should be carried out and who should

---

*Both casebooks (The Mentor Teacher Casebook, edited by Judith H. Shulman and Joel A. Colbert, and The Intern Teacher Casebook, edited by Judith H. Shulman, were developed by the Far West Laboratory for Educational Research and Development and copublished by the Laboratory and the ERIC Clearinghouse on Educational Management. Copies, at $8.00 and $8.50, respectively, are available from the Clearinghouse.

do them. An evaluation system that contributes to teachers' growth and is compatible with a professional view of teaching will have the following characteristics:

1. Teachers are observed in their classrooms more than once or twice a year. Observations are sufficiently frequent to capture teachers' complete instructional repertoires.
2. The results of classroom observations are supplemented with data from self-evaluations, assessments of student work and progress, peer review, and other sources.
3. Evaluation criteria are flexible to account for variations in teaching behaviors across grade levels, subject areas, and different types of students. Rather than simply noting the presence or absence of specified teaching behaviors, evaluators look at teaching in its context, including instructional goals.
4. The evaluator is well qualified—in Wise and Darling-Hammond's words, "a highly expert observer, skilled in subject area and pedagogical matters and familiar with the classroom context."
5. Administrators collaborate with teachers in selecting evaluation criteria, designing evaluation methods and tools, and deciding instructional goals.

In their study of school districts that had effective teacher evaluation practices, Wise and others (1985) found that the distinguishing feature of these districts' approaches was the more professional role of teachers in instructional design and delivery. By involving expert teachers in teacher supervision, these districts were able to increase greatly the time and expertise devoted to the process. The districts "addressed the dual functions of evaluation—monitoring general teaching quality and improving specific teaching performances—by dividing evaluation responsibilities between principals and expert teachers."

Evaluation by Peers

Ward and her colleagues (1985) note that the move to teacher professionalism underscores the importance of persons in the profession accepting responsibility for the quality of its membership. This argument for peer evaluation, "coupled with the move to a staged teaching career, has fostered the use of skilled teachers as evaluators as well as coaches of less skilled teachers."

In the remainder of this section we examine peer evaluation programs operating in Toledo, Ohio, and Orange County, Va., and an initiative to establish peer review in several school districts near Albany, N.Y.

Toledo, Ohio. The Intern and Intervention Plan in the Toledo Public Schools is one of the most advanced and effective peer evaluation efforts in the nation. A cooperative effort of the school district and the Toledo Federated Teachers, the Toledo plan "gives teachers the controlling voice in establishing teaching standards, training and screening new teachers, and identifying new and experienced teachers who need intense assistance," say Ward and her colleagues.

The program matches interns (first-year teachers) with consulting teachers who have at least five years' experience and meet other criteria of excellence. Consulting teachers are released from classroom duties and receive, in addition to their regular salaries, annual stipends of $2,500. Each works with six to eight interns at a time. Three years is the maximum a teacher may serve in this capacity.

Consulting teachers work with the interns during only the first year of their two-year probationary period. During the second year, responsibility for evaluation passes to the principals, who use the same standards and criteria as those used by the consulting teachers during the first year, say Waters and Wyatt (1985), two consulting teachers in the district. They point out that "there have been no instances in which an unsatisfactory rating was given in the second year, a fact that attests to the effectiveness of the first-year screening by the consulting teachers."

Duties of the consulting teacher include assessing interns' teaching skills, helping them set goals for improvement, providing training activities, conducting observations and follow-up conferences, and advising and assisting the interns as needed. In December and March of each school year, the consulting teacher makes recommendations to the school board concerning the interns' future employment.

In addition to the intern component, the Toledo plan has an intervention program that assists nonprobationary teachers performing in an unsatisfactory manner. Each school's principal and teachers' union building committee cooperate in identifying teachers needing assistance. Following action by the Toledo Federated Teachers' president and the assistant superintendent for personnel, a consulting teacher is assigned to work with the poorly performing teacher. Dismissal procedures, when called for, are the responsibility of district administrators.

Toledo's principals, fearing an infringement of their traditional management rights, fought the plan when it was proposed, but now most of them support it enthusiastically. According to Waters and Wyatt (1985), the plan's effectiveness has won over its detractors. During the five years before the plan was implemented in 1981, only one new teacher was terminated. In contrast, seven interns were denied contract renewal during the first four years after responsibility for evaluating new teachers shifted from principals to the teacher consultants.

According to the district's assistant superintendent for personnel, William Lehrer:

> We get consistency, we get competent people closely matched in training to the teachers they are assigned to, and at last we have a way to assist teachers who are experiencing difficulties, without the usual confrontation with the union.

The benefit for the Toledo Federation of Teachers, according to its president, Dal Lawrence, is "that Toledo teachers can now show the public that they care about quality and that they will not tolerate unacceptable performance."

Orange County, Va. At about the same time Toledo's educators launched their plan, the Orange County Public Schools implemented a peer evaluation program that replaced annual teacher evaluations. In contrast to a teacher evaluation system, which exists primarily to identify incompetent teachers, Orange County's Assessment for Professional Development program focuses on assisting the competent 98 percent of the staff to improve their instructional effectiveness.

Before implementing its program, the district identified 15 performance indicators of effective teaching. The program was then designed to give each teacher five years and 30 observations in which to demonstrate his or her proficiency with the indicators.

"Orange County educators," states Edwards (1986), "recognized that the success of the assessment program depended on the feedback given to teachers." To provide this feedback, 35 teacher-observers were trained and provided with released time. Because of differences among the elementary, middle, and secondary school schedules, the observers were assigned to groups of teachers that varied in size: 16 teachers per observer at the secondary level, 8 at the middle, and 4 at the elementary.

Principals, who receive the same training as the teacher-observers, are involved in this program as facilitators and assessors. By reading, rating, and reviewing the observation reports, the principal is able to monitor each teacher's performance and thus guide the teacher's effort in perfecting his or her teaching skills.

The principal's ratings also serve as a check on the teacher-observers.

"Indeed," says Edwards, "the teaching staff's acceptance of the classroom observer as a non-critical, non-evaluator was directly related to the principal's ratings of classroom observation reports."

The district's staff development director conducts monthly seminars for principals on procedures for rating the observations, focusing on one performance indicator each month.

Another facet of this innovative program is that teachers who have demonstrated their proficiency with a performance indicator are appointed as teacher-models. In addition to demonstrating a particular professional practice for other teachers, these teacher-models also assist and guide first-year teachers and conduct workshops in their areas of expertise.

After the program had been in effect for two years, the district surveyed its teachers and found that 84 percent were confident the reporting system would accurately reflect their teaching performance and that 81 percent felt better about the job they were doing.

Edwards (1986) explains why administrators have also responded favorably to the program:

> With teacher-observers conducting formal observations and documenting teacher performance, principals have more information, earlier in the school year, to make instructional and personnel decisions. When problems or staff development needs are discovered, principals have teacher-observers and teacher-models available to provide the individual assistance teachers need. In addition, the staff development director's monthly rating and documentation seminars help establish the principal as the instructional leader and "effective teaching" authority in each school.

Albany, N.Y. Peer review is an essential means of improving the quality of teacher evaluation, according to two reports, issued in 1985 and 1986, by three cooperating organizations in Albany.

In 1985, the Select Seminar on Teacher Evaluation, involving nine master teachers and nine school administrators from 18 school districts near Albany, was sponsored by the Capital Area School Development Association; the Evaluation Consortium, School of Education, State University of New York at Albany; and the Greater Capital Region Teacher Center.

Building on the success of the first seminar, the following year's seminar brought together teams of teachers and administrators from six school districts to develop innovative practices that could be implemented by the participating schools.

Among the first seminar's recommendations is "that the emphasis in teacher evaluation be shifted away from accountability and toward the professional development of teachers." To achieve this purpose, "teachers must begin to evaluate other teachers on a regular basis using systematic peer review and assume major responsibility for evaluation."

Referring to Lortie's (1975) characterization of teaching as "a strange profession that works in a cellular, privatistic, and conservative environment called the classroom," the seminar "strongly recommends that the profession begin to change this structure of cellularity through frequent, informal peer reviews among teachers."

Among the action steps that the seminar proposed are the following:

- Each district should establish a meaningful districtwide policy on professional evaluation by instituting a professional seminar designed to do so. Consciously competent teachers should design and direct that seminar and take leadership in composing and installing district policy on teacher evaluation.

- Each district should identify a cadre of consciously competent teachers who will be trained as teacher evaluation specialists. The district should establish the resources and evaluation training structures required by district policy.

- Each district should ensure that trained teachers who perform evaluations are not required to do so as an added responsibility, but as a portion of their professional day, and that they receive appropriate, meaningful compensation.

- Workshops in classroom observation should be routinely scheduled and required of all new staff members at all levels.

- The only record of such observation and feedback should be documentation that the observation took place. No record of teacher discussion should be kept. Formats for observation should be developed by teachers.

At the second seminar, in 1986, participants put theory into practice by developing workable plans of action. Each school district outlined a program for teacher evaluation tailored to meet the particular needs of its teachers, administrators, and school board. The programs—incorporating varying degrees of observation, consultation, and supervision by peers—were implemented, at least in pilot phase, in fall 1986.

Participants also discussed problems that concern the implementation of teacher evaluation for professional growth. Toward the building of trust between administrators and teachers, for example, the report states that, "either through formal negotiation or through informal agreement, the present power and responsibility relationships within the evaluation process" should be realigned "to permit teachers to participate in their own evaluations and in the professional growth of others." Stereotypical definitions of the boundaries between teachers" and administrators' roles must be discarded. "Leadership should not be based on position; instead it should be based on knowledge and ability."

Throughout the seminar, the report states, every building administrator participant was anxious to form a cooperative partnership with teachers—a partnership that would permit a greater degree of sharing with teachers in the evaluation process and that, in essence, would provide the administrator with a more efficient and supportive institution in which to perform his or her many other tasks.

Conclusion

As several school districts have found, peer review programs are one workable solution to the chronic problem of teacher evaluation. Peer evaluation enlists teachers' commitment to enforce rigorous standards of performance at the same time it contributes to teachers' growth and sense of professionalism.

Some administrators in these districts were at first reticent to share a responsibility that tradition has assigned exclusively to them, but they have been won over by the programs' results. Teachers have demonstrated that, if empowered and trained to do so, they can effectively monitor one another's performance. These self-policing efforts, however, supplement rather than replace the role of administrators in the evaluation process.

Perhaps the most significant contribution of peer review plans is that they unite teachers and administrators in the effort to ensure quality teaching. In traditional teacher evaluation practices, administrators impose performance standards on teachers, who react, predictably, in self-defense. Peer evaluation, on the other hand, ensures that those standards are mutually arrived at and enforced. Teachers and administrators approach evaluation as allies instead of adversaries.

Teacher Participation in Decision Making

The preceding three sections outline structures that increase teachers' influence over the school improvement process, the methods and content of their own professional development, and the performance assessment process. Indeed, one goal of the structures that make up the collaborative school is to increase teachers' professional responsibility and authority.

"If the schools are to compete successfully with medicine, architecture, and accounting for staff, then teachers will have to have comparable authority in making the key decisions about the services they render," states the Carnegie task force, which goes on to say that teachers must be free to make or influence

... decisions concerning such things as the materials and instructional methods to be used, the staffing structure to be employed, the organization of the school day, the assignment of students, the consultants to be used, and the allocation of resources available to the school.

One Principal's Efforts To Involve Teachers

Despite the need to increase teachers' autonomy, no profession—and certainly not teachers in a public education system—can exercise complete freedom of choice over its work. A balance must be struck between teachers' professional freedom and responsibility, as Barth (1980) explains well in his account of his principalship in an elementary school in Newton, Mass.

At his first faculty meeting, Barth set the limits on his teachers' freedom of professional judgment by making a distinction between goals and means:

> In matters of *goals*, the school board, superintendent, principal, parents, and students have considerable, legitimate interest—and say .... It is not acceptable for a teacher to make unilateral decisions about what shall be taught, be it reading, writing, arithmetic, self-confidence, or independence. Not in a public school system. The determination of goals must come from a consensus within the school community.

On the other hand, he told the teachers that questions of educational *means* were best determined by them. "Teachers are trained and experienced in making these instructional decisions, and they derive enormous professional and personal satisfaction from doing so."

In return for this instructional latitude, Barth's teachers were required to respect the way their colleagues taught and to be accountable for results.

"At least twice a year," states Barth, "I would expect each to provide, through careful pupil evaluation, written evidence that the teaching methods and materials he or she had chosen were working."

When Barth came to the school it was bitterly polarized and beset with tensions. As he set about establishing "a school culture that is adult, supportive, professional, cooperative, and humane," his efforts to share power with teachers contributed greatly to the school's renewal.

A significant step was to give teachers control over a portion of the budget. Each year his school system entrusted about 10 percent of each school's budget to the principal for instructional purposes. Barth in turn entrusted to his teachers the expenditure of these funds. Each teacher received $400 or $500 to spend as he or she saw fit. For schoolwide expenditures, such as a movie projector, a committee of teachers made the decision.

Barth "found that teachers entrusted with an instructional budget behave as they do with their personal budgets—they become highly resourceful, responsible, and frugal." Giving teachers control over their own budgets had an unexpected side effect that further moved the school's culture in the direction Barth wanted it to go.

The budget system led to "a dramatic cross-fertilization of ideas among the staff. Instructional responsibility, backed by purchasing power, fosters experimentation, discussion, and cooperation by bringing into the school a constant flow of widely assorted new materials, books, and activities, all of which are cheaper if shared."

Another set of structures Barth utilized to involve his teachers in school decisions was "those tired old workhorses, the committee and the coordinator." He "found that teachers are quite willing to work on a school problem through the committee structure if a committee is small enough so that each member has an opportunity to influence its deliberations and if members feel the ultimate decision rests with them and not with outside authorities."

The formal appointment of subject-area coordinators, Barth observes, makes it easy and legitimate for one teacher to help another, thus overcoming the common taboo against such help (it suggests that one is better than the other).

In addition to fostering collegiality and the sharing among teachers of responsibility for one another's problems, the committees and coordinators also set limits on other teachers.

As Barth notes, "Setting limits on one's peers is perilous. Yet when teachers have legitimate authority, sanctioned by principal and faculty, they find the courage to make demands on their colleagues in one instance and to comply with their colleagues' demands on them in another."

Quality Circles*

Many important ideas originally used in industry have been adopted by educational institutions to enhance their effectiveness. Implementation of these concepts in schools has rarely taken place without some unforeseen influences on other parts of the organization, especially on educational management. The application of Theory Z to the school organization creates definite alterations in basic school structures. One prominent outworking of this theory—the quality circle—illustrates how this importation of new ideas from industry can influence educational management.

According to Ouchi (1981), quality circle members consist of a small group of people (6-12) with a common work interest, meeting voluntarily about one hour a week with administrative encouragement. Facilitators train the members of these circles in group process and problem-solving techniques. Following this training, the quality circle members work at identifying, documenting, and recommending solutions to problems within their work area and range of authority. The key principle inherent in quality circles is that the people performing a job can best diagnose problems in their work and recommend feasible solutions.

*The authors appreciate the contribution of Patrick O'Connor to this section.

Quality circle members are trained to use a variety of specific processes to help them share the power to influence decisions. Briefly, these techniques include brainstorming, voting for consensus, cause and effect analysis, data gathering and analysis, decision analysis, generating solutions, presentation techniques, evaluation, and communication/group process training.

The implications for educational management are many. Administrators need not rely exclusively on rule elaboration, close supervision, disciplined compliance, and centralized decision making to improve teacher performance. Instead, quality circles can help to unite teachers around school improvement efforts.

The process makes use of one of the organization's most valuable assets—human resources—to improve the flow of ideas and increase morale. Management benefits not only from innovative ideas provided by inhouse experts, but also develops management styles that can increase performance.

Unlike other participative management approaches where decision-making responsibility has actually shifted to the group, quality circles do not circumvent preexisting management structures. Although the quality circle members may choose a problem and a solution, they recommend the solution and allow the administrator to make the final decision. Although principals benefit from teachers' expert input about school-related issues such as curriculum matters, principals do not surrender their authority.

Perhaps one of the most important effects that quality circles have on educational management is that the process encourages informal and formal organizations within the school to become one and the same. For example, the teachers' lounge, often a place where grievances are aired outside the formal organizational structure (such as staff meetings), could become a place where concerns are discussed and resolved.

According to two recent studies (Elvins 1985; Rafaeli 1985), participants in quality circles perceived that their influence over their jobs grew significantly. Hawley (1984), describing the outcomes of quality circles in one school district, notes that "the enhanced relationship between teachers and administrators is something everyone sees."

Some school districts have adapted the quality circle concept to fit the unique environment of education. One such adaptation is the Professional Analysis Teams used in the Auburn School District in upstate New York.

According to Malanowski, Kachris, and Kennedy (1986), one departure from the traditional quality circle program is that Auburn's principals have their own team instead of participating in teams with teachers. At each school the teacher team was given jurisdiction to address any problem that affected their jobs. Similarly, the principal team was authorized to address problems related to their responsibilities as administrators.

Before the Professional Analysis Teams were implemented, Malanowski and her coauthors say, Auburn's teachers distrusted their principals, who in turn distrusted the superintendent and felt isolated from the district's administration. Not only have the teams put into action several practical solutions to problems they identified, but participants also report better communication among all levels and greater respect for their expertise.

A number of other structures that facilitate participation by teachers in instructional and governance decisions have been utilized in schools over the years. Whether the format is that of a curriculum council, an advisory committee, or a quality circle, it is important that the arrangement both take advantage of teachers' professional expertise and facilitate their cooperation and sharing.

Although all the strategies discussed above increase teacher involvement in the decision-making process, none diminishes the principal's role. The principal still leads the school, but he or she does so, according to Hall (1986), by involving the entire staff in setting and accomplishing the school's goals. "The importance of the principal's leadership has not changed, but the necessary leadership behavior is different."

Conclusion and Implications

If many schools continue to be structured so that teachers work in isolation from one another—detached from school improvement and uninvolved in one another's professional growth—it is not for lack of alternatives. Across the country educators have fashioned imaginative programs that encourage teachers to work together, pooling their expertise toward such goals as developing new instructional programs, evaluating school outcomes, and improving their professional skills.

None of the practices described in this chapter can be termed a revolutionary departure from the typical school organization. That is to say, principals are still ultimately responsible for leading schools and teachers still teach, for the most part, in their individual classrooms. Nevertheless, the changes these practices introduce go far toward overcoming the isolation, fragmentation, and lack of harmony between teachers and administrators that prevail in many schools.

A major benefit of the programs reviewed here is that they involve cooperation between teachers and administrators. Principals may work with teachers on school improvement teams, or may encourage and support teachers' cooperative professional development. Whether principals participate in these activities directly or not, their role in fostering a school climate that favors collegiality and norms of ongoing improvement is crucial.

Indeed, the key actor at the school level in initiating and facilitating collaboration is the principal, who must provide the support—time, resources, and encouragement—necessary to sustain teachers' collegial interaction. Similarly, districtwide programs require the superintendent's initiative and persistent commitment.

Two different philosophies appear to guide the collaborative programs reviewed in this chapter. In one category are programs that assign certain experienced and well-qualified teachers to special roles, wherein they help administrators run the school or they assist or evaluate other teachers. Some observers have criticized these programs for perpetuating a hierarchical system of control and decision making in schools because the teachers placed in these positions become simply another set of authority figures.

Along this line, Mary Hatwood Futrell, president of the National Education Association, in a "Statement of Support with Reservations" appended to the Carnegie Forum on Education and the Economy's task force report, expressed concern about the lead teacher concept: "It suggests that some teachers are more equal than others."

Originating in a different philosophy are programs that foster cooperation among all teachers, such as collegial observation programs and school improvement teams. Advocates of the latter approaches say they are more compatible with the norms of a profession, whose members share responsibility for quality performance.

Even these supposedly more egalitarian programs, however, assign some teachers more responsibility than others. Moreover, programs that capitalize on real differences among teachers—such as mentor plans that link experienced teachers with colleagues who are beginning their careers—can hardly be considered inconsistent with the principles and goals of the teaching profession.

Chapter 4

Introducing Collaboration in Schools

In Chapter 3 we reviewed a number of practices and programs— ranging from school improvement teams to teaching clinics—that encourage norms of collaboration. In this chapter we will consider ways of introducing such programs into the schools.

Developing and introducing new practices can be a collaborative process, involving teachers, principals, and (depending on the scope of the program or structure) administrators at the district and state levels. However, collaboration on such a large scale may not always be feasible. Teachers may initially be reluctant to work in close cooperation with their principal, and administrators and policy makers at the district and state levels may be hesitant to embark on programs that appear to involve expending funds that taxpayers are unwilling to provide.

Although support at the district level certainly makes it easier to implement collaborative programs and structures, such support is not absolutely essential. In its absence, the principal still has considerable ability to encourage collaboration on his or her own.

In the following paragraphs we discuss ways in which the principal can introduce collaborative practices without relying on support from the district. Considerations involved in the principal's use of a collaborative leadership style are also addressed. We also look at elaborate efforts to collaborate that require a considerable amount of cooperation among personnel at the school, school district, and perhaps even state levels.

In between these comprehensive, districtwide strategies and the efforts principals can undertake on their own are a set of approaches, limited in scale to a particular school site, but still involving cooperation with and support from the districts' central office. These modest approaches are the subject of the fourth section. Next, a variety of considerations involving planning, financial and other resources, and training needs are addressed. The two final sections discuss the legal obstacles to collaborative structures and the need for district level administrators to involve principals in planning programs that assign increased responsibility to teachers.

With collaboration, as with any reform, it is helpful to know what others have done. Therefore, this chapter includes numerous examples of schools and school districts that have implemented collaborative practices. As these examples show, a variety of circumstances can provide the impetus toward collaboration; a diverse set of strategies can be used to bring about collaboration; unanticipated problems can arise when a school or district first begins to adopt collaborative practices; and creative, dedicated leadership makes the difference in overcoming these problems.

The Principal's Role

The principal is in the best position to influence a school's norms. As Kelley (1980) notes, the principal is most responsible for the climate of the school and for the outcomes of productivity and satisfaction attained by students and staff members. The simple truth is that others respond, directly or indirectly, to what the principal does as well as to what he or she does not do.

Because the principal's role in shaping a school's norms is so important, districts should take considerable care in matching the right principal with the right school. Bird and Little (1986) go so far as to say that "a principal can be assigned and supervised effectively only if district administrators go to a school, study its current condition, negotiate the assignment of a principal whose skills and experience apply directly to the present and intended condition of that school, and work directly with that principal to follow through."

The principal who wishes to encourage collaboration in his or her school can make use of a number of strategies, including advising teachers on their practice of teaching, running interference for teachers who desire to interact with one another, building collaborative processes into existing school structures, and modeling effective procedures of classroom observation and teacher evaluation.

Advising Teachers

One step a principal can take toward instituting collaborative norms is to be available when teachers need help in dealing with their classroom problems (of course, this assumes the principal has the skills needed to actually provide meaningful help). Doing so requires both tact and perseverance, inasmuch as teachers may be reluctant to admit that they have problems and may be skeptical about the principal's ability to solve them.

Once staff members come to see the principal as a leader who can help with their teaching problems, the rewards will be worth the effort required to reach this goal. When teachers grow accustomed to asking for and receiving useful advice from the principal, they become more receptive to the idea of asking one another for advice.

Both Rosenholtz (1989) and Bird and Little (1985) found that schools characterized by a high degree of cooperation among the staff were also characterized by a high degree of interaction between staff members and principal—with the latter kind of cooperation setting the stage for the former.

In addition to suggesting ways in which teachers can improve their teaching, the principal who wishes to promote collaboration must make sure that faculty members have the resources needed to make collaboration feasible. For example, a principal may decide to encourage the practice of having teachers plan lessons together. In that case, classes must be scheduled in such a way that teachers have time during the school day to meet.

The same applies when teachers wish to observe each other teach. The schedule must permit one teacher to be free while the other teaches, and vice versa. Both teachers must also be free at the same time to discuss the results of their observations.

Glatthorn (1984) recommends organizing peer observation teams at the end of the school year prior to the initiation of the teams so that the school master schedule can reflect these observing and conferring needs.

In some instances, principals can use substitute teachers to give regular teachers more time for working together. Corbett and D'Amico (1986) point out, however, the potential drawbacks of this approach: "Teachers mistrust substitutes, feel more competent than the stand-ins, and regard time away from students as time stolen from teaching."

One way principals can alleviate the problems posed by using substitutes is for the principals and their assistants to act as replacement teachers. Bruce Wells, principal of North High in the Worchester (Mass.) Public Schools, reports that he and his assistants have frequently stepped in to teach for faculty members participating in study teams at the University of Massachusetts. As Ruck (1986) points out, this practice helps to cut costs and also helps to keep principals in touch with students and the classroom environment.

It may well be that, in most schools, the principal cannot take time away from other activities to serve as a replacement teacher. Ruck says that most of the principals she interviewed would like to spend more time in the classroom but believe they cannot do so and still take care of their other obligations. Yet, it is difficult to see how a principal can function effectively as an instructional leader if he or she is denied the time to engage occasionally in instruction.

The principal's role as a support person need not be limited to removing barriers that impede collaboration among faculty members; the principal can also provide incentives that serve to recognize and reward such collaboration.

Ruck (1986) suggests that, when allocating funds for new materials, preference might be given to teachers actively engaged in collaborative practices. Similarly, when allocating funds for field trips, preference might be given to those trips that involve two or more teachers working together on a project.

Other rewards can also work as incentives to promote collaboration. As Ruck points out, "The message 'You're doing a great job' is not one that teachers hear often."

Simply complimenting teachers for their efforts at working together can serve as a powerful reinforcer, she says.

Corbett and D'Amico (1986) suggest that principals can facilitate improved teaching by employing what Peters and Waterman call "management by wandering around." Instead of relying solely on formal channels of communication to keep track of staff performance, the manager who employs this technique learns what staff members are doing and stimulates desired behavior through daily circuits around the work place.

Management by wandering around would seem to be particularly appropriate for principals who desire to encourage collaboration in their schools. When the principal engages in frequent informal exchanges with teachers that are focused on instructional matters, teachers are encouraged to engage in such exchanges among themselves.

Patience is an important commodity in a school introducing collaborative practices. Ruck (1986) drives this point home by borrowing an analogy from Seymour Papert (author of *Mindstorms: Children, Computers, and Powerful Ideas*, New York, Basic Books, Inc., 1980). When introducing a new program, a programmer expects to encounter "bugs." This doesn't mean the program is a failure; it only means that the bugs must be eliminated.

Similarly, when collaborating for the first time, teachers can encounter unexpected difficulties. This doesn't mean their efforts to interact are ineffective; it only means that the bugs must be ironed out. The principal who clearly explains this process to his or her faculty, emphasizing that initial difficulties in trying out new techniques will not be equated with failure, may find that teachers quickly become emboldened to try those new techniques.

Modifying School Structures

A quick way to get at the heart of collaboration is to encourage teachers to work with one another. Indeed, Schmuck and Schmuck (forthcoming) suggest that the principal has more power over modifying the structures and procedures of the school than he or she has over modifying the norms of the school. Rather than becoming frustrated at being unable to change a school's norms, the principal can simply institute structures that promote cooperation.

One such structure is the faculty meeting, which, say the Schmucks, provides a variety of opportunities to foster collaboration. First, the staff could be encouraged to submit, well in advance of the meeting, issues they feel should be considered. The principal could then use this input in shaping the meeting's agenda. Consequently, the meeting would have a shared agenda—one that addresses the concerns of the principal and of the faculty.

Second, the agenda could be distributed to faculty members well before the meeting. In this way, they would have an opportunity to discuss the issues with one another beforehand.

Third, the principal can involve the faculty in running the meeting. Instead of having the principal chair the meetings, the task can be rotated among the faculty members.

Although none of the steps suggested above is particularly daring, together they can help transform the faculty meeting from an instrument through which the principal promulgates policy into an instrument through which the faculty as a whole, with the principal as leader, develops policy.

The faculty committee is another vehicle that can be used to encourage collaboration among the staff. If the committee members perceive that they are actually expected to study a problem and come up with solutions and if they perceive that their recommendations will be taken seriously, then the committee will actively work together and—in the process—encourage norms of collaboration.

Barth (1986) writes that, when he was a principal, he provided time at the beginning of each faculty meeting to highlight teacher achievements. He also rotated the location of faculty meetings so that each teacher had an opportunity to serve as host, sharing with the rest of the faculty unique features of his or her curriculum or classroom activities. A variation of this approach, practiced by a principal described by Ruck (1986), is to set aside time at faculty meetings for teachers to describe inservice programs they have attended, innovations they have introduced into their classrooms, and the like.

Observing and Evaluating Teachers

In Chapter 1, we listed what Little (1982) called the critical practices of adaptability that were encouraged by norms of collaboration. One of these critical practices is providing teachers with frequent and useful critiques of their teaching. In a school with highly developed norms of collaboration, such critiques can frequently be supplied by a teacher's colleagues.

Where such norms have not already been developed, the principal must take the lead in conducting frequent and useful classroom observations and evaluations of his or her staff. As we have seen, such assistance by the principal encourages teachers, in turn, to assist one another.

Requirements for success. It should be emphasized that frequency of evaluation is not a sufficient condition: For evaluations to be useful, teachers must perceive that the evaluations actually help them to improve in their work.

According to Bird and Little (1985), reciprocity between the principal and the teacher must prevail if observation and evaluation for instructional improvement are to be meaningful. Such reciprocity requires the following conditions:

1. The observer must *assert* the knowledge and skill needed to help a practitioner of a complex art.
2. The teacher must *defer* in some way to the observer's assertion, that is, the teacher must accept the observer's claim to possess the skill and knowledge needed to help the teacher.
3. The observer must *display* the knowledge and skill which he or she necessarily asserts.
4. The teacher must *respond* to the observer's assertions, at least

by *trying* some change in behavior, materials, role with students, or perspective on teaching.

5. The observer's performance must *improve* along with the teacher's, and by much the same means: training, practice, and observant commentary from someone who was present.

The principal who hopes to use observation and evaluation to help teachers improve must expect to expend considerable time and energy in doing so. In those schools studied by Bird and Little that had strong observation and evaluation programs, the principals had done considerable reading to improve staff knowledge of teaching and of observation and evaluation practices, and teachers had taken the time to attend training sessions in these areas. In one junior high school, each of the 45 teachers was observed by the principal or vice principal for five successive days in the fall and five successive days in the spring.

After a principal has successfully established observation by administrators as a tool for helping teachers to improve, the path has been cleared for introducing peer observation. Bird and Little found that in schools where teachers thought that observation by the principal had helped them to improve, they were receptive to observing and being observed by their colleagues.

Again, time and energy are necessities; teachers cannot be expected to meet the requirements of reciprocity outlined above unless they have some preliminary training in observation and in providing useful commentary on what they have observed.

Peer coaching. According to Garmston (1987), the first step in implementing a peer coaching program is the selection of a coaching model—technical, collegial, or challenge—best suited to the particular goals of the school and the particular needs of the school's faculty. After a model has been selected, the principal can support peer coaching by demonstrating that he or she considers coaching important, providing a focus for coaching activity, providing training for coaches, and modeling positive coaching behaviors.

Garmston mentions several practical ways in which principals demonstrate the importance they attach to peer coaching and model positive coaching behaviors. For example, they can provide time at faculty meetings for teachers to share their ideas about coaching and allow coaching teams to get together during time that would otherwise be spent on full-scale faculty meetings. And principals can model positive coaching behaviors by soliciting staff critiques of faculty meetings (in effect, letting himself or herself be coached by the faculty) and by "shadowing" other principals. That is, the principals of two schools can take turns observing each other in action and coaching each other.

Peer observation. What Garmston says about the principal's role in peer coaching also applies to the principal's role in peer observation. It is important for the principal to demonstrate that he or she considers peer observation important, to provide a focus for observations, to provide adequate training, and to model positive observation behaviors.

Ruck (1986) encourages principals to implement peer observation procedures that follow the clinical supervision model, where the emphasis is on reinforcing a teacher's strengths rather than pointing out his or her weaknesses, and where the individual being evaluated has a voice in deciding what aspects of his or her classroom performance are to be evaluated. In the early stages of a peer observation program, when teachers may be nervous about observing and being observed by one another, the principal can help put together pairs of teachers who will feel comfortable with each other. If conflicts arise, the principal can act as a counselor to help the parties work out their differences.

Bird and Little's (1985) principle of reciprocity, mentioned earlier, has applications that go far beyond the areas of observation and evaluation. To effectively introduce collaborative norms into a school, a principal must be an effective teaching leader. This means that he or she must assert and display the mastery of teaching and the leadership that entitle him or her to lead the staff through a period of change. Similarly, the staff must accept and respond to the principal's efforts to initiate changes. And, in the overall effort to institute norms of collaboration, the principal's skills at leadership must grow along with the teachers' skills at teaching.

Empowering Teachers

Shortly after Barth (1987) became a principal, he received a memo from a veteran teacher indicating his intention "to stay out of school until the deplorable and illegal fire safety standards have been corrected." Barth could have denied that the situation was serious enough to warrant any action, or he could have promised to do something about it himself. But he did neither. Instead, he offered to let the teacher develop his own plan for improving the school's fire safety standards and pledged his support for any plan the teacher might devise.

The teacher went on, says Barth, to create "an incredible school fire safety system." He met with individual teachers and classes to discuss the dangers posed by fire hazards, held fire drills for individual classes and for the school as a whole, and even arranged for a nearby church to provide shelter should a fire break out during the winter months.

The teacher, the school, and Barth himself all derived benefits from entrusting fire safety to the teacher. Barth was free to devote his time to other duties. The school enjoyed the benefits of a more thorough fire safety program than Barth would have had time to develop on his own. And the teacher received recognition for having done something to solve one of the school's pressing problems.

This example illustrates a number of important points. First, many teachers have leadership qualities that can be tapped for the benefit of the school as a whole. Second, teachers are more likely to use those leadership qualities when they can be applied to problems of particular concern to them than when they are applied to problems of concern only to the principal. And third, teachers are more willing to use their leadership qualities when they are given the authority to develop their own plans and the support needed to implement them.

Of course, not all teachers are deeply concerned about fire safety. But many teachers are concerned about particular facets of the way the school is run. Some might want to upgrade the science curriculum.

Some might want to assemble reading materials. And some might want to revamp the library. In any case, the school is best served when the individual teacher or teachers most interested in a given problem are given the authority to solve that problem.

The principal and the faculty can find additional guidelines and practical suggestions for implementing collaborative practices in *Ventures in Good Schooling: A Cooperative Model for a Successful Secondary School*, developed jointly by the National Education Association (NEA) and the National Association of Secondary School Principals (NASSP). This booklet is intended to serve as a practical tool to help teachers and principals examine their responsibilities to create a quality instructional program at the school site. Drawing on a large body of research, *Ventures* provides indicators denoting characteristics of effective schools.

The NEA and the NASSP encourage principals and teachers to use the booklet together as a means of determining where their school stands and where they want it to go. In essence, *Ventures* provides a framework in which principals and teachers can work together to promote school improvement—and, in the process, to foster collaboration among teachers and between teachers and the principal.

Preparing for a Collaborative Style of Leadership

The shift from an authoritarian or a bureaucratic mode of leadership to a collaborative one is not an easy step for many school administrators to take. One mistake is to change one's leadership style too quickly. The administrator should take time to adapt his or her style of leadership to the situation in the school, taking into account such factors as teachers' unity, expertise, and readiness to assume increased responsibility for decisions. Some teachers, comfortable in their isolation and autonomy, will feel threatened when the principal suddenly announces they must now critique one another's teaching or take a more active role in deciding school issues.

One effective way to prevent teachers' anxiety from mounting is to precede the introduction of collaborative leadership and structures with an effort to clarify and emphasize the school's purpose.

Rosenholtz (1989) found that teachers' anxiety was lowest and their cooperation in school improvement was greatest when they clearly understood and rallied around their school's goals. With their attention and energies focused on a common objective, teachers were more open to criticism from their peers and more willing to help each other improve their practice.

Once the faculty has embraced the school's mission, then the principal can explain that the most effective means for marshalling the school's resources toward fulfillment of that mission is a collaborative approach, which will involve a change in everyone's roles.

Leading Versus Imposing

At all stages, the wise principal is careful to distinguish between leading the way toward collaboration and imposing collaboration on the faculty. Wildman and Niles (1987) describe the essential nature of collaboration in the following terms:

> Collaboration naturally complements autonomy. Freedom to direct one's own learning is a vital aspect of collaboration. Collegial groups must be flexible in their composition and purpose. They must form and disintegrate based on the needs of individual teachers. And it is teachers who must decide on the specifics of their collaboration. Control of collegiality, either externally or hierarchically, is antithetical to the basic concept. Professionals cannot be forced to be collegial.

According to Fullan (1985), "Successful change involves pressure, but it is pressure through *interaction* with peers and other technical and administrative leaders" (his emphasis).

Sharing his recipe for the development of a teaching clinic similar to Pittsburgh's Schenley's High School Teacher Center, Davis (1986) advises administrators to adopt a caring attitude:

> Personal talks with individual teachers exploring this new dimension in professionalism are important. Group feedback sessions to monitor the feelings of participants, as they experience the trials and tribulations of growth, are essential.

Will an administrator who adopts a collaborative style be perceived by colleagues and some subordinates as weak or ineffective? Perhaps so, initially.

Shakeshaft (1987), speaking about issues facing women administrators, notes that those who manage from a collaborative framework do so in a system that stresses the value of competitive individualism and personal achievement at the expense of community goals. Conceding the reality of such a system, effective women leaders often report that they first establish themselves and then introduce participatory styles, Shakeshaft says.

While preparing their staff members for collaborative approaches, women leaders acknowledge that they were mistaken, at first, for weak administrators.

"Nevertheless," Shakeshaft asserts, "the research offers overwhelming evidence that women's collaborative style works best and over the long haul is instrumental in women being rated as effective leaders."

Blending Collaborative and Assertive Approaches

The collaborative approach to leadership is not intended to work in all schools all the time. Kenneth Tewel, principal of Brooklyn's George Westinghouse Vocational and Technical High School, explains that schools go through several stages of development requiring different leadership styles. Quoted in "The Urban School Principal: The Rocky Road to Instructional Leadership" *(Carnegie Quarterly,* Winter 1986), Tewel points out that some situations call for authoritarian approaches, whereas others call for a more collaborative style.

The problem is that many principals get stuck in one style of leadership and run into trouble:

> A lot of leaders can't shift their mode of leadership to fit changed circumstances. They carry their battlefield mentality into less critical phases of

the school's evolution. As a result, they are unprepared to assume a more moderate, collaborative mode once the school is past crisis. This can create fissures within the school community, blocking further innovation.

Long after a school's faculty members have taken on increased responsibility for school improvement and their own professional growth, some situations will still call for directive, assertive leadership.

Mann (1986) points out the flaws of school improvement efforts that rely strictly on voluntary participation by teachers. He advises administrators to operate with a complete repertoire of leadership strategies—the soft, voluntary techniques, as well as the hard, assertive approaches.

"In the absence of cooperation and where reasonable persuasion does not avail, the exercise of leadership may end with the assertion of power, that is, the leader requiring the follower to do what the follower would not otherwise have done," Mann says.

Again, we are reminded that collaboration is but one means to achieve quality schools, and that, depending on the circumstances, there are other, equally valid means to achieve the same end. Further, those means are not mutually exclusive. Principals can delegate responsibility for some issues to teachers and on other issues insist that teachers follow their direction.

Comprehensive Strategies

Thus far we have focused on the principal's role in encouraging collaboration and leading the collaborative school. In this section we discuss methods of encouraging collaborative endeavors that require extensive initiative and support from the school district's central office.

The experiences of schools that have successfully implemented collaboration suggest collaborative norms can be introduced into a school in either of two ways.

One is to adopt a comprehensive approach: assessing the school's culture and the ways in which that culture does or does not serve the needs of the school's population, identifying norms that should be changed, and determining specific steps to take to improve those norms.

The other strategy follows a more limited, indirect approach. The principal identifies a particular problem confronting the school and solicits the help of the staff (and, in some instances, the students) in solving that problem. By thus involving the entire school community in working together to solve one problem, norms of collaboration are encouraged.

In this section we consider four models of school improvement that exemplify the comprehensive approach. The merits of the indirect approach are the subject of the following section.

Reaching Success Through Involvement

Reaching Success through Involvement (RSI) is a strategy for initiating change at the school building level developed at Vanderbilt University. By 1986, RSI had already been implemented in 14 schools in five states and was being introduced in 28 additional schools in five other states.

As explained by Furtwengler (1986), RSI is a long-term (12 to 36 month) strategy for school improvement. Its 11 steps run from recognition by the principal and assistant principals of their responsibility for the school's overall effectiveness, through formation of a planning council, development of inservice programs, collection of data to assess progress being made, and (at the end of each year) election of new members of the planning council.

Perhaps the most striking features of RSI are its focus on continuous planning and action throughout the school year, and its emphasis on involvement of participants from all segments of the school community.

The planning council (consisting of administrators and faculty members) and a student leadership group take part in a three-day retreat to focus on leadership training and problem-solving activities. At the retreat, task forces (with student representation) are formed to solve specific school problems. Each task force holds at least four half-day meetings during the school year to assess the progress it is making and determine what further work must be done.

Although RSI is a strategy focusing on improvement at the school level, it clearly requires strong support from the central office if it is to work. It is difficult to see how RSI could work without the expenditure of considerable time by both administrators and faculty. Asking faculty members to use their "spare" time for the purpose would place an unfair burden on them and likely would incur their resentment. And, if the time is to come from their regular working hours, substitutes must be provided or additional staff must be hired.

Organizational Development

Another comprehensive strategy for school improvement that encourages collaborative practices is organizational development (OD). As explained by Schmuck and colleagues (1985), OD is aimed at improving the ability of the subsystems of a school district to change themselves.

Schmuck and his colleagues base their strategy on four postulates:

● First, schools are constituted of components—individuals, facilities, books, and so on—which are further organized into subsystems.

● Second, "as living systems, schools are goal-directed. Usually, however, the goals are stated so vaguely by school personnel that they cannot be recognized even when they are being reached." In many cases, a school's stated goals may be at variance with those goals that the school's activities actually promote. To the extent that this happens, the school must either live with the contradiction; close off communication, which advertises the ambiguity; change its proclaimed goals; or change its behavior.

- Third, schools, like other living systems, display varying degrees of openness in communication. Administrators may communicate with school boards, curriculum committees may be in touch with outside experts, and teacher organizations may be in contact with teacher organizations from outside the school or the district. Such contacts bring outside influences and ideas to bear within the organization. "Strain within schools occurs when one subsystem (such as the curriculum division) brings new practices into the district and another subsystem (such as a school building staff) resists trying the new practices."

- Fourth, schools maintain many resources and plans that at any one time are not being used. While these plans "will inevitably include a number of irrelevant or even potentially deleterious practices, a school can be adaptive only if it encourages the emergence of whatever resources exist for optimizing its educative functions."

Given the four postulates outlined above, it is not surprising that OD attempts to improve the ability of schools to change themselves through clarifying school goals, improving communication among various elements of the school community, and tapping the school's unused resources. To do so, OD employs the services of an outside facilitator, who works closely with the district's central office and the principal and faculty members.

Three features of OD are especially worth noting:
- First, OD emphasizes the importance of developing a plan that fits the situation at a particular school. The facilitator must be satisfied that a particular plan will work before implementing it and must be prepared to monitor it and modify it as necessary.

- Second, OD includes plans for terminating the consultation process when those services are no longer needed, and for institutionalizing the changes that have been introduced. This includes training a cadre of school personnel to continue the work after the facilitator has gone.

- Third, OD places a strong emphasis on encouraging and developing collaborative processes. Facilitators train participants in ways of better expressing themselves and listening to one another. The facilitators, through group discussions with participants, attempt to identify group norms, distinguishing between those that simply reflect current practices and those that describe how members of the school community would like things to be. For example, teachers may practice norms of isolation simply because that is the way things have always been done and each teacher is reluctant to be the first to do things differently. Through group discussions, each teacher may find that he or she is not the only one who would like to engage in more collaborative practices. Once group support for such practices becomes apparent, participation in such practices becomes much easier.

Although OD, like Reaching Success through Involvement, typically employs outside facilitators to work with members of a school's population, many OD principles and methods can be employed usefully by administrators who have no formal training in the subject. The handbook by Schmuck and colleagues provides considerable information along those lines.

Staff Development for School Improvement Program

A third program designed to encourage collaboration at the school building level is Wayne State University's Staff Development for School Improvement Program (SDSI), which involves approximately 15 school districts. The program, as described by Hall (1986), involves a six-step process:

Readiness. After a facilitator from the program meets with the principal and faculty of the school to explain the program and answer questions about it, the faculty members vote on whether or not to participate. The project moves forward only if 70 percent or more of the staff vote to participate.

Needs assessment. The facilitator leads the staff through diagnosis, brainstorming, and ranking activities to select school goals. After one or two goals have been selected by consensus, planning team members are selected to work on the building's plan.

Writing the plan. With the help of the facilitator and the principal, the planning team writes up the plan, which specifies objectives, activities to be completed, persons responsible for the activities, evaluation plans for each objective, and costs. The plan is then discussed and modified by the faculty members. Finally, the plan is examined, modified (if necessary), and approved by project staff members at Wayne State University.

Implementation. A building-level team consisting of the principal and faculty members implements and coordinates activities called for by the plan. These usually include school visits, workshops, classroom observations, student reward systems, curriculum development by committees, conferences, and materials preparation.

Evaluation. In this step, formative (including implementation evaluation) and summative data are collected to monitor progress toward the school's goal.

Reassessment and continuation. The facilitator and the school's staff members examine the year's accomplishments, decide what they wish to accomplish in the following year, and develop a new plan for that year.

According to Hall, evaluations of the first three years of the SDSI process found that 82 percent or more of the teachers in each school observed improvements in knowledge, skills, communication, and participation in decision making.

Hall notes that, for this staff development program to succeed, the principal must emphasize that the project's goal is to encourage ongoing growth. If the principal does so and actively encourages teachers to share ideas with one another, the norms of collaboration established through the program will continue after the original program has been completed.

Pittsburgh's Teaching Clinic

Another ambitious program to break down the barriers that isolate teachers is the Schenley High School Teaching Center in the Pittsburgh Public Schools. In the previous chapter we described the center's operation; here we highlight its origins.

"In the late 1970s," says Henderson (1986), "Pittsburgh's public schools were stuck in a political quagmire."

The school board was wrapped up in arguments over court-ordered desegregation. And parents—unhappy over the way desegregation was being handled and believing that the quality of education in the public schools was deteriorating—were transferring their children to private schools.

In the period from 1980 through 1985, the situation improved markedly. According to Henderson, in 1981 almost half the elementary and middle schools in the district scored below the national norm in academic achievement tests; by 1985, all those schools scored above that norm. The high school dropout rate—35 percent in 1980—was down to 21 percent by the end of 1985. And during the period from 1983 through 1985, 3,400 students whose parents had transferred them to private schools returned to the public school system.

What caused the turnaround? Richard C. Wallace, Jr., the district's superintendent, was widely acknowledged as chief architect of Pittsburgh's educational rebuilding effort. But Wallace did not accomplish the task on his own.

First, Wallace and his staff, with the assistance of educators at the University of Pittsburgh, surveyed the community—including children, parents, teachers, and administrators—to see what was on people's minds. Having pinpointed the problems to be faced, the superintendent took his results to the school board. The board then chose to back Wallace and his staff in developing a number of programs designed to improve teaching and learning.

These included MAP (Monitoring Achievement in Pittsburgh), a program to establish districtwide educational goals; PRISM (Pittsburgh's Research-based Instructional Supervisory Model), used for training and evaluating teachers; and the Schenley High School Teacher Center.

A number of factors contributed to making the Pittsburgh Public Schools' improvement program a success. First was the leadership provided by the district's superintendent. Second, the school board was willing to back the superintendent's efforts at educational reform. Third, he surveyed all the important elements in the community to ascertain their perception of the district's needs, instead of merely imposing his own program on the district. Fourth, instead of trying to improve teaching by removing inferior teachers, Wallace initiated a strong effort to improve the performance of all district personnel.

Wallace involved all the interested parties in shaping Pittsburgh's programs. For example, secondary school teachers were involved in planning the Schenley High School Teacher Center from the very beginning. And finally, the local union, an affiliate of the American Federation of Teachers, was willing to work closely with the district to implement its programs.

Modest Approaches

Although Reaching Success through Involvement, Organizational Development, the Staff Development for School Improvement Program, and the teaching clinic developed by the Pittsburgh Public Schools differ from one another in many important respects, they share one common element: All are comprehensive programs intended to produce far-reaching changes in the ways in which administrators and teachers within a school or a district approach their profession.

Many schools and districts perceive no need for such sweeping changes; in some cases efforts at initiating such changes can even be counterproductive. Kelley (1980) notes that, where levels of satisfaction with the current situation are high, changes are unlikely to produce many positive results. If proposed changes would require resources that are not available, things may be better left unchanged.

Although school administrators may determine that sweeping changes such as those envisioned in the RSI strategy or in the Pittsburgh Public Schools program are unsuitable for their needs, they may find that other, less sweeping changes may help solve specific problems. At the same time, those changes may help to strengthen norms of collaboration. Of three examples that serve to clarify the point, two are reported by Lieberman and Miller (1984), and the third is based on our interview with a principal.

Reforms Lead to Collaboration

The faculty and administration at Big City High School (the fictitious name Lieberman and Miller give to a school they studied) felt the need to develop alternative programs to service the school's diverse student population. In collaboration with a nearby major university, Big City High established a teacher center in the school building. At first, the center was headed by a university staff person; later, control was given to one of the high school's teachers, who was freed from regular classroom duties.

The teacher center eventually became a meeting place for teachers who wanted to plan for change in present structures and procedures. According to Lieberman and Miller:

> Teachers came to the Center individually and in groups. They came to read, to reflect on their teaching, and to plan together. After three years, the Center is very much a part of the school. It has become an important school institution.

It is important to note that the teacher center succeeded because it met a perceived need of the faculty: a place where teachers could work together to plan strategies for meeting the needs of their students.

Lieberman and Miller's other example is based on what happened in a medium-sized, urban school district when teachers became involved in districtwide improvements and their own professional development.

There was a consensus among principals and faculty members that the district lacked remedial materials in language arts and reading that elementary teachers could use in their regular classroom instruction. A group of principals and teachers sought the support of the assistant superintendent of curriculum for a project involving teachers in materials development. In response to their request, the district hired 45 teachers to work for two weeks during the summer on developing materials for classroom use. Three pilot schools developed their own methods of introducing the materials into the classroom.

One comment by the assistant superintendent is particularly worth noting: "The district level curriculum staff served as consultants to the schools on an invitational basis. That is, the district staff responded to expressed staff needs rather than taking a leadership position." Six months into the project, the assistant superintendent indicated that it was generally viewed as a success.

It appears that both the teacher center at Big City High School and the project for developing remedial materials in the urban school district strengthened norms of collaboration. Together, teachers planned for improvement at the teacher center, and teachers worked together to develop materials for remedial instruction. But in neither case was the reform introduced for the purpose of increasing collaboration as such. Rather, the reforms were a response to the perceived needs of the teachers in matters regarding instruction and curriculum. In the process of addressing those needs, collaboration took place.

North High

Another school that incorporated collaborative practices is North High in the Worchester (Mass.) Public Schools. Bruce Wells, the principal, told us the school traditionally served a student body consisting primarily of middle class whites with strong educational backgrounds who intended to go on to college. The goals and practices of North High's faculty reflected these demographic considerations.

In the 1970s, Worchester's demographics changed considerably and the composition of North High's student body changed accordingly. Instead of serving a student body consisting primarily of white, middle class students with strong educational backgrounds, North High found itself serving a student body consisting primarily of disadvantaged students from minority groups, many of whom lacked the strong educational backgrounds of their predecessors.

While the composition of the student body changed radically, the composition of the faculty did not. Teachers who had spent their entire careers helping students prepare for college found it difficult to adjust to working with students who were poorly grounded in the basics.

Wells saw that something needed to be done to help the faculty adjust to their changing circumstances. He found help in the Massachusetts Coalition for School Improvement—a branch of John Goodlad's National Network for Educational Renewal, discussed in the previous chapter.

Through the coalition, Wells was able to provide faculty members with the opportunity to attend symposiums at the University of Massachusetts conducted by Goodlad and his associates. At subsequent faculty meetings, teachers returning from the symposiums were able to share their experiences with the rest of the staff.

Work with the coalition is serving as the catalyst for a number of other changes at North High that are encouraging faculty self-renewal and improving teaching and learning. North High began working with the University of Massachusetts Medical Center to develop a magnet program on health and science. Faculty planning groups began working on setting curriculum development priorities. And North High's faculty began working with the faculties of the high school's primary feeder middle schools to work out mutual problems.

Wells suggested that the key to successfully involving faculty members in collaborative endeavors is finding a hook that will make it worth their while to spend the extra time and effort needed to make such endeavors a success. For the faculty at North High, the hook was the opportunity to participate in symposiums led by noted educational leaders such as Goodlad. Initially, faculty members might have participated in the program simply for the thrill of working in person with such individuals; having done so, however, they returned to North High and engaged in collaborative activities with their colleagues.

Planning, Resources, and Training

As we have seen, collaborative structures vary from comprehensive, districtwide strategies to simple changes in the way faculty meetings are run. Among the variables that govern the choice of a structure appropriate for a particular district or school are the perceived need for collaboration, the readiness of the faculty and administration for change, and the availability of any additional resources that will be needed to implement the structure. What may be desirable for one setting may not work well in another. And what may be desirable on its merits may, regrettably, be impractical, given the district's or school's financial resources.

Needs Assessment and Selection of Collaborative Structures

A beginning step is to assess where the district or school is on the continuum between isolated and collaborative. How often do teachers interact on educational issues? Do they have experience working together on school or instructional improvement? Do they observe one another teach and share strategies for improvement? Answers to questions such as these can help in assessing structures that would be appropriate.

Teachers and administrators who have had little experience with collegiality may need to be convinced of its benefits before new practices can be initiated. In such a case, it is best to start on a small scale, involving those personnel, including union representatives, who show interest. Their involvement in planning collaborative structures is itself a step toward collegiality and a participative management style. Further, say Ward and her colleagues (1985), such involvement "demonstrates the seriousness of the school/school district's commitment to recognition and use of teachers' expertise."

A major drawback of many traditional teacher evaluation and professional development programs is that they are not linked with broader district and school improvement efforts. The goal in implementing a collaborative program should not be to produce collaboration for its own sake. Rather, it is best first to identify an important need in the school or district and then to select, with teachers, a collaborative activity that will fulfill that need. The activity and the collaboration it fosters are but means to achieve the instructional improvement or other goal desired.

Once the purpose is clarified, selection of an appropriate method can be made. To ascertain the track record of a particular collaborative approach to school improvement or professional development, a planning team could consult the research literature. In other schools where the program or structure has been implemented, what results have been obtained? How do teachers and administrators in those schools judge the program's effectiveness? Are data available that link the program to student achievement? If answers to these questions are not available in print, the team could visit schools operating the program to obtain the information first hand. Insights gained from site visits can not only help in deciding whether this structure will work for you, but also how it can best be implemented.

Time

All parties should realize that introducing norms of collaboration is a process that requires time. Formal programs such as RSI and OD are designed to run for anywhere from one to three years. It may very well take that much time before such programs show visible results in the form of increased teacher collegiality, involvement in school governance, and faculty-management harmony. It may take even longer before those changes have any discernible effect on teachers' instructional effectiveness and student achievement. Hence, patience is a requisite in the effort to foster collaboration.

Introducing collaborative norms also takes time in another sense, as Bird and Little (1986) attest: "time for teachers to study, analyze and advance their practices; time for principals, department heads, and teacher leaders to support improvement; time for faculties to examine, debate, and improve their norms of civility, instruction, and improvement."

Such time must come from somewhere. It is both unfair and unrealistic to expect teachers to somehow find the time for collaborative activities *and* continue to do everything they are expected to do already.

While acknowledging the difficulties involved in furnishing teachers with the time needed for collaborative endeavors, Wildman and Niles (1987) stress the importance of overcoming those difficulties:

> Finding more time for teacher growth obviously involves increased costs, but time-efficient staff development efforts that do not produce teacher learning are clearly not cost effective. Time for teacher learning is one of the most important investments a school system can make to maintain and improve quality educational programs.

According to the National Governors' Association's report, *Time for Results*, schools typically spend about one-tenth what private industry devotes to development of personnel.

In a discussion of the time required for a collegial observation program, Roper and Hoffman (1986) argue that the real problem is one of priorities:

> Convincing the powers that be that teachers are professionals who learn best from one another is the central issue. In the financial crunch facing so many school districts it would seem easier to "sell" a program that does not require high priced consultations, expensive materials, and disruption of classes than the more typical inservice experience that often requires all three. Strange as it seems, districts will often pay the price for the legitimacy of the expensive "expert" rather than put those resources into using their own staff as experts. Lack of time is a symptom, not a cause, for the more basic problem of lack of support for collegiality.

In a study of teacher participation in school-level improvement programs, Dawson (1984) compared the relative effectiveness of using non-instructional time (planning periods, lunch, and before and after school) and non-discretionary time (scheduled for classroom instruction, faculty or department meetings, and inservice activities). Use of non-instructional time had several disadvantages:

> The length of time available was usually brief—one hour or less. Teachers felt rushed, could not block out other concerns and concentrate on planning, or were tired. Consequently, some planning sessions were relatively unproductive. Furthermore, teachers considered this non-instructional time discretionary and sometimes resented being asked to relinquish it.

Non-discretionary time, on the other hand, required more resources but had several advantages:

> Usually, longer blocks of time were available for uninterrupted work. Participants were often more relaxed and productive. Teachers perceived the allocation of time to a new project as evidence of administrator commitment and were encouraged to continue their involvement.

Dawson reports that non-discretionary time had to be used judiciously to avoid overreliance on substitutes. To reduce the amount of time required for the programs, schools spread the process over a longer period, reducing the frequency of meetings; reduced the extent of participation, such as assigning initial planning to a core group; and replaced larger groups with multiple smaller groups that could meet at separate times.

Finances

In financial terms, the cost of implementing collaborative programs varies widely from program to program and district to district. The more comprehensive and elaborate the program, the more it can be expected to cost.

Judy A. Johnston, director of the Pittsburgh Public Schools' Schenley High School Teacher Center, places the cost of running the school as a teacher center (over and above the cost of a normal high school operation) at about 1.5 million dollars a year—or about 1.5 percent of the district's overall budget. Stressing that most of this cost is for the salaries of replacements (full-time district employees) for teachers attending the center, Johnston suggests that other districts might be able to find ways of achieving the same objectives while avoiding that cost.

Other costs that derive from Schenley's operation as a professional development center include salaries for the director and her assistant, clerical salaries, seminar presenters' fees, and ongoing inservice.

Kay Mitchell, director of the Charlotte-Mecklenburg (N.C.), School District's Teacher Career Development Program, estimates the program's cost at about 4 million dollars out of a district budget of 225 million dollars (or about 1.7 percent).

The Toledo Public Schools' Intern/Intervention Plan in the 1986-87 school year cost that district $448,000 more than a traditional teacher evaluation program would have cost, according to Robert D. Corcoran, Toledo's executive director of personnel. This expenditure, consisting primarily of salaries for 17 consulting teachers, represents less than one-fourth of 1 percent of the district's $200 million annual budget.

Two factors should be kept in mind when evaluating costs such as those outlined above. First, they are the costs of large-scale, district-wide programs; school-level innovations such as involving faculty in school improvement teams may require no financial expenditure. And second, programs such as the Schenley Teacher Center replace other, conventional staff development programs that also cost money.

A district can seek external sources of funding for programs that might capture people's imagination. Johnston explained that Schenley's startup costs of approximately $400,000 were borne largely through grants of various types.

If a district can't compensate teachers for all the time they spend on a collaborative activity, partial payment is better than none. The Auburn, N.Y., School District decided to compensate participants in its Professional Assistance Teams for four of the six hours they spend each month at team meetings (held when school is not in session so as not to interfere with the educational process).

Training

Another consideration in planning collaborative structures is the need for training in such skills as problem solving, communication, and observation of classroom teaching. Although in some instances consultants must be hired, again a concerted effort can be made to identify capable trainers among the district's or school's staff.

Especially important is the proper training of teachers who are given responsibility for assisting other teachers. Davis (1986) reports that during the first three years of the Schenley Teacher Center's operation the leadership cadre received about 60 hours of training in addition to the initial basic training. The elements of this advanced training are as follows:

1. Teaching analysis skill development
2. Conferring skills
3. Group process
4. Group management/peer group feedback
5. Personality styles
6. Problem-solving approaches
7. Introspection/when teachers face themselves
8. Adult learning theory
9. Effective schools research
10. Helping and collegial relationships
11. Effective questioning strategies
12. Eliciting and receiving feedback
13. Alternative methods of data collection
14. Conflict resolution/adult depression
15. Teacher diagnostic summary review

Instructional chairpersons and other key teachers in the Pittsburgh Public Schools are now being trained in these same areas. As Davis says, "It's truly important to have a cadre of teachers who are competent in coordinating their own professional development."

According to Garmston (1987), good training for peer coaches "uses the best available information about adult learning; provides teachers with theory, information, and demonstrations; addresses teachers' concerns about giving and receiving feedback; and helps teachers develop and refine specific coaching skills."

Peer coaching is a sufficiently complex skill that training should be provided to participants on an ongoing basis through refresher courses and follow-up sessions.

When the Auburn School District in upstate New York implemented its Professional Analysis Teams based on the quality circle model, the district committed itself to an extensive training effort to make sure the program worked. Malanowski, Kachris, and Kennedy (1986) point out that whereas quality circles in industry deal largely with matters of statistical quality control, problems in education are complex and their solutions are not obvious. For this reason, the training of Auburn's Professional Analysis Teams focused on solution development. Participants were taught how to identify possible solutions and to evaluate and gather data.

Additional training was needed as the teams proceeded. At first, if team members identified several problems related to a common theme, they combined the problems in the attempt to find an overall solution.

For example, say Malanowski and her colleagues, the problem with students being removed from class for special help was linked to the problem of poor study skills and remediation activities. Team members had to be given special training to think not in common themes but rather in terms of dividing an issue into its various parts.

Preparing for Unforeseen Problems

Superintendents, principals, and teachers who introduce collaborative structures into their schools should realize that it is unlikely everything will work out exactly as planned. As is the case when introducing any innovation, unforeseen needs will arise that require modification of programs.

Kay Mitchell, director of the Charlotte-Mecklenburg (N.C.) School District's Teacher Career Development Program, discussed in the previous chapter, says that the program originally proceeded on the assumption that outstanding teachers with the most experience would be best suited to the role of mentor teachers. Subsequently, it was discovered that good teachers with only 5 to 10 years of experience made the best mentors. These teachers were closer in age to the individuals they were mentoring, and thus their relationships were more comfortable. Further, they were still sufficiently close to their own experiences as beginners to retain a vivid memory of what new teachers face.

Another unforeseen problem the Charlotte-Mecklenburg program encountered was that some teachers who were chosen to be mentors because of their exemplary performance actually turned out to be "tormentors," as Mitchell put it. When put in a position of power over interns, they became excessively critical and abused their authority in other ways as well.

The fine-tuning of another teacher mentor program is described by Huie, Brown, and Holmes (1986), who evaluated the Intern-Mentor Program of the District of Columbia Public Schools after its first year of operation. One problem concerned the number of interns (10) originally assigned to each mentor. Because mentors showed signs of burnout, the evaluators recommended that the number of interns per mentor be reduced to 8. Because the mentors spent much time locating or making instructional materials for their interns, Huie and his coauthors also recommended that the district supply mentors with improved office support and teaching resources.

Psychological Barriers

Some teachers and administrators will oppose collaboration, if not outwardly at least by passive resistance, because they are unable to deal with the emotional issues that arise from opening their work to others' critiques, or from (in the case of administrators) sharing their responsibilities and authority. Indeed, fear, defensiveness, insecurity, and other emotional reactions are among the strongest barriers to collaboration in schools. Resistance grounded in such psychological factors can be difficult both to detect and to overcome.

Opposition to collaboration is rarely overt. In recent years, collegiality has become widely regarded as an important aspect of teachers' professionalism. Consequently, to avoid seeming unprofessional, teachers who cannot cope with the realities of interacting with their peers must find subtle ways of undermining those interactions.

Grimmett (1987) found that such sophistry was common among principals and teachers in a school district seeking to implement peer coaching. The practitioners spoke persuasively about the advantages of peer interaction, yet failed to structure opportunities for practice and feedback, "admitting that time constraints, peer incompatibility, professional threat, and interpersonal defensiveness, in most cases, essentially rendered their participation in the peer-coaching process minimal."

How can planners of collaborative programs increase the chances that personnel will actually participate, rather than merely pay lip service to the programs? Here are some helpful guidelines:

- Avoid all kinds of pressure on individuals to participate; coercion causes resentment and encourages hypocrisy. It is especially important to avoid a bandwagon mentality; everyone may jump on, but some will jump off once the spotlights are dimmed.

- Instead of exhorting or pressuring people to participate, let the program sell itself, through modeling and sharing examples of success.

- If incentives are offered to participants, don't make them so attractive that everyone will volunteer, whether or not they intend to follow through on their commitments; for the same reason, don't impose sanctions on those who refuse to participate.

- Involve prospective participants in the planning and designing stages of the program or activity, and make adjustments in response to reasonable apprehensions that are voiced.

- Allow participants honestly to register their feelings, without fear of censure, at all stages of the program.

- Appoint as program coordinators and trainers people who can effectively model such traits as personal security, self-confidence, humility, openness to criticism, and honesty.

Legal Obstacles

In some parts of the country, school districts that try to implement new structures will discover that first they must free themselves from the straitjacket of state legislation. This is the case in Louisville, Ky., where, as Olson (1986) reports, the Jefferson County Public Schools must petition the state to waive or modify requirements that would prevent the district from creating professional development schools similar to Pittsburgh's teaching clinic. Perhaps as educators demonstrate their resolve to improve school structures, policy makers will see fit to relinquish some of the control over local education that in recent years has been hoarded in state capitols. As one means of restoring control to the local level, Finn (1986) proposes:

... a sort of treaty that does not yet exist in many places, but that could be started via a simple provision of state law permitting individual districts—even individual schools—to waive other laws and regulations as long as their students do not fall below minimum performance levels.

Another hurdle that might have to be overcome before some collaborative practices can be introduced in schools is the collective bargaining contract. If a district's current contract limits management's freedom to structure the work environment, a new contract may have to be negotiated before certain kinds of collaborative programs can be introduced. The union may be willing to relinquish some of its control of the work environment in exchange for the district's commitment to involve teachers in decision making.

Involving Middle Managers

When administrators at the district level plan programs that will expand teachers' roles, principals and other site administrators will most certainly want to be involved in the planning and be allowed to assess the programs' impact on their roles. Rodman (1987) describes the controversy that erupted in Rochester, N.Y., over implementation of a mentor teacher program negotiated between the school district and the local teachers' union, without input from the principals of the affected schools. In response, the Association of Supervisors and Administrators of Rochester filed suit against the school district and the local teachers' union, arguing that the program assigned to mentors supervisory and administrative tasks which properly belonged to principals and their assistants.

Rodman quotes Patricia S. Carnahan, president of the local administrators association, as saying that she is not opposed to the concept of a mentor-teacher program, but she is "opposed to the way the district implemented its program. Administrators' needs have been pretty much ignored."

Carnahan's comments highlight the need to involve all affected parties in any change process. Having district level administrators and teachers work together without involving principals is as antithetical to the principles of collaboration as it would be for district level administrators and principals to work together without involving teachers.

On the other hand, middle managers, fearing that their authority will be undermined, may oppose out of hand any initiative that assigns some of their traditional responsibilities to teachers. Dal Lawrence (1987), president of the Toledo Federation of Teachers and architect of the Toledo Intern/Intervention Plan, writes candidly about the program's origin:

> It should come as no surprise that Toledo principals and supervisors were dead set against these changes. It took nine years of "protracted consideration" before their objections were overrun. I choose that term carefully. Principals and supervisors were overrun, not convinced. We had a turf problem, plain as can be. Authority would be undermined, or altered, it was argued, and certainly a school would never be the same if principals lost any part of their authority base. In fact, that was the whole point, wasn't it? We didn't want schools run the same way.

Within a year after the program was implemented, principals conceded its success and saw that their fears were unfounded. "Instead of losing face, or control, as had been feared, principals found more time to offer a variety of other support services," Lawrence comments.

Conclusion

In several respects, introducing collaboration into a school or a school district resembles any other effort at school reform. The essential ingredients in such efforts are an accurate assessment of the school's or district's needs and resources and the ability to enlist the support of all appropriate personnel. Programs launched before the needs and resources of the school or district are assessed or that fail to win the support of the personnel involved will almost certainly end in failure.

These similarities are true, however, only of the implementation of schoolwide or districtwide programs that induce teachers and administrators to collaborate on such tasks as school improvement, curriculum development, or peer review. Although formal efforts to encourage collaboration may be appropriate in some schools and districts, other educators may prefer a less structured approach.

A single teacher, for instance, can take the first step simply by consulting with a colleague about a problem in his or her classroom. A principal who wants to encourage the faculty to interact about instructional matters can set an example by routinely seeking the advice of individual teachers or of the faculty as a whole. These efforts incur no costs—except psychological ones for those who risk challenging norms of isolation—and they are the most direct route to the goal of a collaborative work environment.

Even the structured approaches can be considered successful only to the extent they encourage educators to engage in frequent, informal discussion about the practice of their craft.

Because collaboration ultimately depends on voluntary, informal actions of teachers and administrators, perhaps the biggest obstacle to collaboration in schools is complacency. Teachers and administrators must first be convinced that the isolation of teachers in their classrooms and the top-down management philosophy that ignores teachers' expertise are short-changing both those who work in schools and those who are taught there.

In the absence of such conviction, it will be easy to dismiss collaboration as too time-consuming, costly, or disruptive of the status quo. Perhaps the most important prerequisites for introduction of collaborative norms and practices, therefore, are that the school's principal and a majority of its faculty members share a vision for an alternative work environment and are willing to devote their energies, expertise, and resources to see that vision fulfilled in their midst.

Conclusion

Is the time right for the collaborative school? Optimism appears to be justified. After decades of failed attempts to improve schools through strategies imposed from above, now is indeed the right time to put to use the resources already within the walls of each school—the experience and skills of the teachers and administrators who work there.

We have noted evidence that suggests when the personnel in each school cooperatively help to improve one another's skills and the performance of the school as a whole, a number of good things happen: they enjoy their work more, their skills improve, and they perceive themselves as being more effective. Even more important, according to a small but growing body of findings, student achievement is higher in schools having collaborative settings than in schools where teachers work in isolation from one another.

By its very nature, collaboration is a school site phenomenon, fashioned by the personnel at each school. Therefore, the future of collaboration lies very much in the hands of educators themselves. Will they view it as an option—to be desired or not, depending on the preferences of each school's faculty members and principal—or as a requirement for quality schooling, to be energetically pursued even at high cost? The answer, of course, depends on how convinced educators themselves are about the benefits of collaboration and whether, convinced or not, they are prepared to change ingrained patterns of behavior.

A prerequisite for collaboration is that all parties desire to relate to one another in constructive new ways. Administrators must convey to teachers that their participation in school governance is desired. In turn, teachers who have adopted a combative stance toward management must shed their hostility. Respect and cooperation must flow in both directions.

In addition, teachers must be willing to work together as a team and principals must be both willing and able to define the team's common purpose and give structure to its work. Along with the loneliness and occasional desperation that accompany isolation from colleagues are certain emotional rewards. How ready are teachers to forfeit their freedom from inspection and criticism?

Alphonso and Goldsberry (1982) point out that coordinating professionals in the fluid context of collegial support is a complex task that cannot be done through generating formal rules, or even standardized procedures. Consequently, a collaborative school requires a higher caliber of leadership than does a bureaucratic school.

The question must be raised, therefore, whether collaboration can succeed only in those schools already experiencing able instructional leadership. This question is all the more disturbing because collegial support is more desperately needed in schools that lack effective supervision of instruction and coordination of improvement. It may be that, if collaboration is to take root in such schools, it will be through an act of courage by principals who admit to their own lack of time and skills and aggressively enlist the talents of others to build an effective pattern of instructional leadership.

Principals undoubtedly would find it easier to take such action if educational policy makers would more visibly promote the concept of instructional leadership as a collective activity, not the sole responsibility of principals.

An inherent characteristic of collaborative norms and practices is that they cannot be imposed on a school's personnel by outside authorities. Cooperation and teamwork depend on voluntary effort and frequently require that personal preferences by subordinated to group goals. Whether teachers and administrators in a majority of the nation's schools eventually will decide the benefits of collaboration are worth the material and psychological costs remains to be seen. On their choice depends the success of the current movement to create a truly professional work environment for teaching.

References

Many of these references are indexed in ERIC's monthly catalog *Resources in Education* (RIE). Reports in *RIE* are indicated by an "ED" number. Journal articles that are indexed in ERIC's companion catalog, *Current Index to Journals in Education*, are indicated by an "EJ" number.

Most items with an ED number are available from the ERIC Document Reproduction Service (EDRS), P.O. Box 190, Arlington, Va. 22210. To order from EDRS call 1-800-227-3742 for price information.

Acheson, Keith A., with Smith, Stuart C. *It Is Time for Principals to Share the Responsibility for Instructional Leadership with Others.* Eugene: Oregon School Study Council, University of Oregon, February 1986. OSSC Bulletin Series. ED 267 510.

Alfonso, Robert J., and Goldsberry, Lee."Colleagueship in Supervision." In *Supervision of Teaching*, edited by Thomas J. Sergiovanni. Alexandria, Va.: Association for Supervision and Curriculum Development, 1982. ED 213 075.

Ambrosie, Frank. "The Case for Collaborative, Versus Negotiated, Decision Making." *NASSP Bulletin*, September 1989.

Ashton, Patricia T., and Webb, Rodman B. *Making a Difference: Teachers' Sense of Efficacy and Student Achievement.* New York and London: Longman, 1986.

Bacharach, Samuel B., and others. *Paying for Better Teaching: Merit Pay and Its Alternatives.* Ithaca, N.Y.: Organizational Analysis and Practice, Inc., 1984. ED 280 130.

Barth, Roland S. "The Principal and the Profession of Teaching." *The Elementary School Journal*, March 1986. EJ 337 994.

——. *Run School Run.* Cambridge: Harvard University Press, 1980.

——. "School: A Community of Leaders." Paper presented at annual spring conference of the Georgia State University Principals' Institute, Atlanta, March 4-5, 1987. ED 281 277.

Bebermeyer, Ruth. *Leadership for School Climate Improvement.* Working paper prepared for the Urban Education Network, St. Louis, Mo., March 1982. ED 221 949.

Bird, Tom, and Little, Judith Warren. "How Schools Organize the Teaching Occupation." *The Elementary School Journal*, March 1986. EJ 337 995.

——. *Instructional Leadership in Eight Secondary Schools.* Boulder, Colo.: Center for Action Research, Inc., June 1985. ED 263 694.

Brophy, Jere E. *Using Observation to Improve Your Teaching.* Occasional Paper No. 21. East Lansing, Mich.: Institute for Research on Teaching, Michigan State University, April 1979. ED 173 339.

Capital Area School Development Association. *A View from the Inside.* Report of the Select Seminar on Teacher Evaluation. Albany: State University of New York, January 1986.

_____. *A View from the Inside: A Look to the Future.* Report of the Select Seminar on Teacher Evaluation. Albany: State University of New York, December 1986.

Carnegie Forum on Education and the Economy. *A Nation Prepared: Teachers for the 21st Century. The Report of the Task Force on Teaching as a Profession.* New York: Carnegie Corp., 1986. ED 268 120.

Corbett, H. Dickson, and D'Amico, Joseph J. "No More Heroes: Creating Systems to Support Change." *Educational Leadership,* September 1986. EJ 343 739.

Davis, Lawrence E. "A Recipe for the Development of an Effective Teaching Clinic." Paper presented at the annual conference of the Association for Supervision and Curriculum Development, San Francisco, March 1, 1986. ED 275 028.

Dawson, Judith A. *The Principal's Role in Facilitating Teacher Participation: Mediating the Influence of the School Context.* Philadelphia, Pa.: Research for Better Schools, Inc., April 1984. ED 244 346.

Edwards, Clarence M., Jr. "An 'Effective Teaching' Approach to Teacher Evaluation and Staff Development." *ERS Spectrum* IV, Spring 1986. EJ 338 738.

Elvins, Jane P. "Communication in Quality Circles: Members' Perceptions of Their Participation and Its Effects on Related Organizational Communication Variables." Paper presented at annual meeting of the International Communication Association, Honolulu, May 23-27, 1985. ED 257 153.

Feiman-Nemser, Sharon, and Floden, Robert E. "The Cultures of Teaching." In *Handbook of Research on Teaching,* edited by Merlin C. Wittrock. New York: Macmillan, 1986.

Fielding, Glen D., and Schalock, H. Del. *Promoting the Professional Development of Teachers and Administrators.* Eugene, Oreg.: Center for Educational Policy and Management and ERIC Clearinghouse on Educational Management, University of Oregon, 1985. ED 260 489.

Finn, Chester E., Jr. "Teacher Unions and School Quality: Potential Allies or Inevitable Foes?" *Phi Delta Kappan,* January 1985. EJ 311 705.

_____. "We Can Shape Our Destiny." *Educational Leadership,* September 1986. EJ 343 724.

Flinders, David J. "Teacher Isolation and the New Reform." *Journal of Curriculum and Supervision,* Fall 1988.

Freiberg, H. Jerome. "Master Teacher Programs: Lessons from the Past." *Educational Leadership,* December 1984-January 1985. EJ 311 568.

Fullan, Michael. "Change Processes and Strategies at the Local Level." *Elementary School Journal,* January 1985. EJ 315 744.

Furtwengler, Willis J. "Reaching Success Through Involvement—Implementation Strategy for Creating and Maintaining Effective Schools." Paper presented at annual meeting of the American Educational Research Association, San Francisco, April 17, 1986. ED 274 085.

Garmston, Robert J. "How Administrators Support Peer Coaching." *Educational Leadership,* February 1987. EJ 350 642.

Glatthorn, Allan A. *Differentiated Supervision.* Alexandria, Va.: Association for Supervision and Curriculum Development, 1984. ED 245 401.

Goodlad, John I. *A Place Called School: Prospects for the Future.* New York: McGraw-Hill, 1984.

Grimmett, Peter P. "The Role of District Supervisors in the Implementation of Peer Coaching." *Journal of Curriculum and Supervision,* Fall 1987.

Hall, Burnis. *Leadership Support for Staff Development: A School Building Level Model.* Detroit, Mich.: College of Education, Wayne State University, 1986. ED 275 029.

Hawley, David. *Quality Circles.* Eugene, Oreg.: Oregon School Study Council, University of Oregon, September 1984. ED 248 598.

Henderson, Keith. "Pittsburgh Rebuilds Its Inner-City School System." *The Christian Science Monitor,* January 10, 1986.

Huie, David L.; Brown, Joan W.; and Holmes, Dennis H. *A Study of the Intern-Mentor Program.* Washington, D.C. : Division of Quality Assurance and Management Planning, District of Columbia Public Schools, 1986. ED 279 077.

Kelley, Edgar A. *Improving School Climate: Leadership Techniques for Principals.* Reston, Va.: National Association of Secondary School Principals, 1980. ED 202 120.

Knoop, Robert, and O'Reilly, Robert R. *Job Satisfaction of Teachers and Organizational Effectiveness of Elementary Schools.* 1978. ED 177 719.

Lawrence, Dal. "The Relevance of *Yeshiva* to Public Education: A Union Perspective." *Journal of Law and Education,* Winter 1987. EJ 350 677.

Little, Judith Warren. "Norms of Collegiality and Experimentation: Workplace Conditions of School Success." *American Educational Research Journal,* Fall 1982. EJ 275 511.

_____. "Teachers as Teacher Advisors: The Delicacy of Collegial Leadership." *Educational Leadership,* November 1985. EJ 329 579.

Little, Judith Warren, and Bird, Thomas D. "Is There Instructional Leadership in High Schools? First Findings from a Study of Secondary School Administrators and Their Influence on Teachers' Professional Norms." Paper presented at annual meeting of the American Educational Research Association, New Orleans, La., 1984. ED 263 690.

Lortie, Dan C. *Schoolteacher: A Sociological Study.* Chicago and London: University of Chicago Press, 1975.

Malanowski, Rose M.; Kachris, Peter; and Kennedy, Valerie. "Professional Analysis Teams in Schools: A Case Study." Paper presented at annual meeting of the American Educational Research Association, San Francisco, Calif., April 20, 1986. ED 280 135.

Mann, Dale. "Authority and School Improvement: An Essay." *Teachers College Record,* Fall 1986. EJ 344 595.

Meade, Edward J., Jr. "School-Focused Development of Teachers On-the-Job." Outline of remarks delivered to the Fall Conference of the Council of the Great City Schools, Pittsburgh, Pa., September 20, 1985. ED 268 628.

Metz, Mary Haywood. *Different by Design: The Context and Character of Three Magnet Schools.* New York: Routledge and Kegan Paul, 1986. ED 271 455.

National Education Association and National Association of Secondary School Principals. *Ventures in Good Schooling: A Cooperative Model for a Successful Secondary School.* Washington, D.C.: NEA, and Reston, Va.: NASSP, 1986. ED 272 977.

National Governors' Association. *Time for Results: The Governors' 1991 Report on Education.* Washington, D.C.: Center for Policy Research and Analysis, 1986.

Nelson, Barbara Scott. "Commentary: Teachers Can Be Trusted to Reform Their Profession." *Education Week,* February 25, 1987.

Neubert, Gloria A., and Bratton, Elizabeth C. "Team Coaching: Staff Development Side by Side." *Educational Leadership*, February 1987. EJ 350·643.

Olson, Lynn. "Network for Renewal: Goodlad Seeks Stronger School-University Alliances." *Education Week*, March 18, 1987.

_____. "A 'Teaching Hospital' Model." *Education Week*, November 19, 1986.

Ouchi, William G. *Theory Z*. Reading, Mass.: Avon Books, 1981.

Purkey, Stewart C., and Smith, Marshall S. "Effective Schools: A Review." *The Elementary School Journal*, March 1983. EJ 281 542.

Rafaeli, Anat. "Quality Circles and Employee Attitudes." *Personnel Psychology*, Autumn 1985. EJ 326 322.

Rodman, Blake "Homes for a 'Team of Fellow Professionals': Some Teacher Locals and School Officials Are Reaching for Collaborations Beyond Bargaining." *Education Week*, April 6, 1988.

_____. "New York Lawsuit Highlights Growing Tension Between Principals, Teachers over Their Roles," *Education Week*, January 14, 1987.

Roper, Susan Stavert, and Hoffman, David E. *Collegial Support for Professional Improvement: The Stanford Collegial Evaluation Program*. Eugene, Oreg.: Oregon School Study Council, University of Oregon, March 1986. ED 275 067.

Rosenholtz, Susan J. "Education Reform Strategies: Will They Increase Teacher Commitment?" *American Journal of Education*, August 1987.

_____. "Political Myths about Education Reform: Lessons from Research on Teaching." *Phi Delta Kappan*, January 1985. EJ 311 709.

_____. "Teacher Experience and Learning: Do All the Good Die Young?" Paper obtained from the author.

_____. *Teachers' Workplace: The Social Organization of Schools*. New York: Longman, 1989.

Ruck, Carolyn L. *Creating a School Context for Collegial Supervision: The Principal's Role as Contractor*. Eugene, Oreg.: Oregon School Study Council, University of Oregon, November 1986. ED 276 111.

Rutter, Michael, and others. *Fifteen Thousand Hours: Secondary Schools and Their Effects on Children*. Cambridge: Harvard University Press, 1979.

Sarason, Seymour B. *The Culture of the School and the Problem of Change*. Boston: Allyn and Bacon, 1982.

Schmuck, Richard A., and others. *Handbook of Organizational Development in Schools*. 3rd ed. Mountain View, Calif.: Mayfield Publishing Co., 1985.

Schmuck, Richard A., and Schmuck, Patricia A. "The Cooperative Classroom and School Climate." In *Handbook of Cooperation in Education*, forthcoming.

Sgan, Arnold D., and Clark, J. Milford. "Support Teams for Teachers: The Principal's Role, and How the Team Functions." *NASSP Bulletin*, May 1986. EJ 337 498.

Shakeshaft, Charol. "Organizational Theory and Women: Where Are We?" Paper presented at annual meeting of the American Educational Research Association, Washington, D.C., April 20-24, 1987.

Shedd, Joseph B. *From the Front of the Classroom: A Study of the Work of Teachers*. Ithaca, N.Y.: Educational Systems Division, Organizational Analysis and Practice, Inc., December 1985. ED 280 131.

Showers, Beverly. *Peer Coaching: A Strategy for Facilitating Transfer of Training*. Eugene, Oreg.: Center for Educational Policy and Management, University of Oregon, October 1984. ED 271 849.

Shulman, Lee S. "Teaching Alone, Learning Together: Needed Agendas for the New Reforms." In *Schooling for Tomorrow: Directing Reforms to Issues That Count,* edited by Thomas J. Sergiovanni and John H. Moore. Boston: Allyn and Bacon, 1989.

Snyder, Karolyn J., and Anderson, Robert H. *Managing Productive Schools: Toward an Ecology.* Orlando, Fla.: Academic Press, 1986.

Tewel, Kenneth J. "Collaborative Supervision—Theory into Practice." *NASSP Bulletin,* April 1989.

"The Urban School Principal: The Rocky Road to Instructional Leadership." *Carnegie Quarterly,* Winter 1986.

Wagner, Laura A. "A State Perspective on Teacher Leadership Roles: The Potential of the California Mentor Teacher Program." Paper presented at annual meeting of the American Educational Research Association, San Francisco, Calif., April 16-20, 1986. ED 272 964.

Ward, Beatrice; Pascarelli, Joseph T.; and Carnes, James. *The Expanding Role of the Teacher: A Synthesis of Practice and Research.* Portland, Oreg.: Northwest Regional Educational Laboratory, November 1985. ED 265 160.

Warner, Dee. "Mentor Teacher Pilot Program Acclaimed by Teachers, Administrators in Schenectady, Guilderland, and Rensselaer School Districts." *CASDAIDS Newsletter,* June 1987.

Waters, Cheryl M., and Wyatt, Terry L. "Toledo's Internship: The Teachers' Role in Excellence." *Phi Delta Kappan,* January 1985. EJ 311 713.

Wildman, Terry M., and Niles, Jerry A. "Essentials of Professional Growth." *Educational Leadership,* February 1987. EJ 350 640.

Wise, Arthur E., and Darling-Hammond, Linda. "Teacher Evaluation and Teacher Professionalism." *Educational Leadership,* December 1984-January 1985. EJ 311 588.

Wise, Arthur E., and others. "Teacher Evaluation: A Study of Effective Practices." *The Elementary School Journal,* September 1985. EJ 324 222.

Interviews and Correspondence

Corcoran, Robert D. Executive Director, Personnel, Toledo Public Schools, Toledo, Ohio. Letter to authors. 19 May 1987.

Johnston, Judy A. Director, Schenley High School Teacher Center, Pittsburgh (Pa.) Public Schools. Letter to authors. 11 May 1987.

Mitchell, Kay. Director, Teacher Career Development Program, Charlotte-Mecklenburg (N.C.) School District. North Carolina. Telephone interview, 8 April 1987.

Wells, Bruce. Principal, North High School, Worchester, Mass. Telephone interview, 15 April 1987.